SOMERSET AND DORSET
SWANSONG

SOMERSET AND DORSET SWANSONG

Last Days of a Steam Railway

Bob Bunyar

Cover: "Bude" and "Biggin Hill" head across Midford viaduct with the southbound RCTS special on Saturday 5th March 1966. Don Froud

Rear Cover: Passengers return to the RCTS special before it gets under way from Midford station on the evening of Sunday 6th March 1966.

Frontispiece: "Okehampton" and "Biggin Hill" on the southbound RCTS special at Midford, halted for photographs on the evening of Sunday 6th March 1966.

Title Page: 48706 heads the Great Western Society special south past Midford goods yard on the morning of Saturday 5th March 1966. Don Froud

The author

Bob did not have a railway career, choosing instead to join the Bath Fire Brigade where he achieved thirty one years service before retiring. He is a lifelong railway enthusiast, has been a frequent contributor of articles and pictures to journals both local and national, and is well known to many fellow railway enthusiasts throughout the West Country. For the last thirty years Bob has served as a volunteer on the Swanage Railway, twenty years as a guard. He now works on projects at Harmans Cross and is a key member of the railway's marketing team. Bob is a longstanding member of Bath Railway Society, joining in the "Midland Hotel" days, and it is through this happy association that much material for this book has been gathered.

Publisher's introduction

This is an illustrated account of the closing moments in the life of the Somerset and Dorset Railway, written from the perspective of someone who experienced it at first hand. The author illustrates aspects that have received less attention in previous books and the background to the closure is also briefly covered.

We hope that fifty years and many publications after closure, this book will both interest the informed enthusiast and introduce the Somerset and Dorset to those who never knew the line.

From a publisher's perspective this book marks the addition of a new "portfolio" style, intended to widen the range of our more traditional catalogue.

My thanks to Bob for the initial book, George Mumford for much help in the production stages, Stephen Dent for design work and Peter Barnfield for friendship, inspiration and mentoring over many years.

Simon Castens

WILD SWAN BOOKS LTD.

© 2016 Wild Swan Books Ltd and Bob Bunyar
ISBN 978 0 953877 14 0

Designed by Stephen Dent
Printed by Amadeus Press, Cleckheaton

Published by
Wild Swan Books Ltd.
3A Upper Lambridge Street, Larkhall, Bath, BA1 6RY

CONTENTS

———•◆•———

INTRODUCTION

THERE ARE MANY FILMS, photographs and accounts available today that
record the special and final passenger trains
that operated over the much lamented
Somerset and Dorset line before its closure
from March 7th 1966. However, the various
workings in the days and weeks before the
final closure did not generate the same public
interest and seem to have gone relatively
unnoticed.

In this book I have tried to gather as much
information as possible in order to give
detailed accounts of all the final workings over
the line in addition to information on some
of the more interesting operations leading up
to closure and beyond.

Railways are in my family blood. My
Great Grandfather Edwin Harvey joined the
Midland Railway as a porter in 1873 at
Desford station. Following promotion and
moves to Lowdham, Southwell, Bugsworth
and Hykeham stations, he ended his career as
the longest serving Stationmaster of
Plumtree station near Nottingham. In 1919

The author with his Grandfather on Wellow
Station in 1955.

Stationmaster Edwin Harvey, centre, photographed with his staff at Plumtree station on the Midland
Railway.

he retired and moved to Bath, taking up residence close by the Somerset and Dorset line in Oldfield Park.

My own association with the S&D began at our home in Wellow, I could see the trains passing from our garden and I spent many childhood hours on the station, also visiting the signal box. We frequently travelled into Bath and sometimes to Radstock by train, and when rumours of closure began to circulate my parents decided to move into Bath. I visited Green Park station and spent much time after school on what was locally known as the "tump" a piece of raised ground situated opposite the loco sheds. I often travelled into Bristol from Bath Green Park via Mangotsfield to go train spotting and carried

on all these activities right up to closure.

I made my last journey on a passenger train over the S&D on the Great Western Society Special on Saturday March 5th, and I must admit I had tears in my eyes upon our return to Bath Green Park Station. I had taken an old Kodak box camera with me so I could capture my own images, however when the pictures were developed the prints were not of a very high standard, but they were my personal memento of the day. I lost these prints and their negatives in a house move many years ago and so it has given me great pleasure to assemble this collection of memories and photographs of this famous railway line, with much of the material coming from acquaintances and friendships

Margaret Harvey is seen off on the train to Nottingham in 1951 by her cousin Sylvia Bunyar, the author's mother. The train is formed of red and cream Stanier coaches and the roof of Green Park station can just be seen at top right.

Bertha Clifford, the author's great aunt, standing next to an S&D train at Bath Queen Square station in April 1930. In the background can be seen the station's bonded warehouse.

Bath Queen Square station in 1930, with an S&D train standing in approximately the same position as in the previous photograph.

Richard Dagger

formed over the fifty years that have passed since that final weekend.

I have included workings over the Midland line into Bath which closed at the same time and I have also tried to check all information against known sources. A small proportion of what I have written cannot be backed up, but where this is the case I have made this clear in the text. There are still questions to be answered and hopefully over time further information may yet come to light to fill in any remaining gaps.

I am delighted that I have been able to put my research into a book and I wish to thank Simon Castens for all his help and assistance with this. I am also very much indebted to Tim Bullamore, Tim Deacon, Derek Coles, Keith Barrett, Nick Feast, Keith Fletcher, Mike Standhaft, John Lakey, Peter James, Terry Nicholls, Keith Pfrangley, the Blandford Railway Club, Don and John Froud in addition to anyone else who I have not mentioned who has assisted or provided me with information in compiling this book. In addition Peter Barnfield, Michael Chapman, Tim Chapman, Robert Coles, Geoff Ellis, Nigel Hunt, Julian Peters and Phil Sutters have provided their precious images for which I am grateful.

Uncredited photographs are from my own collection and are published here in good faith. If I have used any photographs without due acknowledgement then please contact me via my publisher so that future editions may be suitably credited.

Above all I would like to thank my very good friend Mike Ware for all the information he has provided and sourced for me, and in particular, for the use of his Dad's notes from his log books. Bernard Ware was a guard on the S & D working right up to the very last day of operation on Sunday March 6th 1966.

Bob Bunyar
Swanage, Dorset. 2015

Chapter One

THE FINAL YEARS & RUN DOWN

ON 27th MARCH 1963 "The Reshaping of British Railways" (The Beeching Report) was published, proposing widespread closure of railway lines and stations across the country. Shown in the list of outright closures on Page 106 were the lines from Bath Green Park to Bournemouth West and Bristol Temple Meads to Bath Green Park. The end of the S&D line, with over 103 route miles in total along with 35 stations, was now to become a reality.

In June 1963 British Railways announced that passenger services over the S&D and Midland line to Mangotsfield would be withdrawn in September. Closure was then cancelled as the Transport Users Consultative Committee was unable to deal with the resulting flood of objections and complaints, and there followed an agonising silence as the Ministry delayed a further decision. Hopes were raised in the following year when the Labour party won the General Election on a manifesto promise to halt all major rail closures, but the axe fell again in June 1965 with an announcement that the line would close that September. Further objections again delayed matters, but finally on Monday 6th September 1965 the new Labour Government, in the shape of Minister of Transport Tom Fraser, announced that both the S&D and the Midland route from Bristol to Bath Green Park would close to all passenger traffic from January 3rd 1966. This was despite their earlier promises, severe crit-

On the 16th May 1959 S&D 7F 53800 heads a mixed freight up the bank just to the south of Midsomer Norton. *Rev. John Sutters, courtesy Phil Sutters*

icism from the unions and representations from numerous organisations and groups. On 23rd December 1965 Barbara Castle became the new Minister of Transport, but she refused to reverse or review the decision. The Western Region announced that the 3rd January would be "D Day" when steam motive power would be completely eliminated from their

region, although subsequent events would see this announcement backfiring, as we shall see in Chapter 2.

In truth, the Beeching Report only served to confirm what was increasingly apparent to those with an interest in the line, the S&D was not seen as part of the future by the Western Region of British Railways.

A Radstock based Jinty tank is providing rear end assistance to the train. It will continue banking as far as Masbury Summit, six miles further on and nearly 600 feet higher, before dropping off and running back down to Radstock. Rev. John Sutters, courtesy Phil Sutters

No Diesels

When the Western Region started to modernise, they introduced diesel services on many lines and branches that were subsequently closed, but no services over the S&D were ever dieselised. In March 1962 there was a reduction in train services in the Bristol Area, including those on the Midland route between Bristol Temple Meads and Bath Green Park via Mangotsfield. Writing about the changes at the time, the Bristol Divisional Traffic Manager Mr D. S. Hart stated: "*In 1959 diesel trains, one of the products of the Modernisation Plan, replaced most of the steam trains in the Bristol area and we made every effort to attract you to them. They were and they still are, faster, cleaner and cheaper to run. The results were disappointing – many of our trains have been running almost empty. The picture has not radically changed since these intensive services were started and we have no alternative but to reduce the number of trains*". His statement concluded by saying "*We must concentrate on running those services which our customers are prepared to support in reasonable numbers and will do all we can to make them as efficient and attractive as possible*". Although the Midland route into Bath did see some regular diesel workings in this period, the Somerset & Dorset remained a wholly steam powered operation and it was increasingly clear that the authorities did not see the line as part of their diesel powered future.

S&D crews were never trained on diesels, so if they were to operate over the line "foreign" crews would have to be used, with a local man in the cab providing route knowledge. Despite this handicap, the line nonetheless saw some diesels on special workings. The first was on 10th May 1958 when the Gloucestershire Railway Society chartered a three car Swindon Cross Country DMU for its "Dorset Rail Tour". This originated at Cheltenham and ran via Gloucester and

Bath driver Trevor Barber watches over his train before departure from Green Park station in July 1960. Caprotti fitted Class 5 44749 is Speke Junction based and probably about to return north with a through express.

Mangotsfield to Bath Green Park, before running over the S&D to Templecombe enroute to Lyme Regis. Not knowing the capabilities of a DMU over the Mendips, the authorities provided an assisting locomotive in the shape of a "Jinty" tank engine at Radstock. In the event this was not required as the unit performed without problem over the steep grades. Fifteen days later a similar formation ran through to Bournemouth on an excursion from Birmingham, but this time no assisting engine was provided. Two other DMU workings followed in 1959, with a final through working from Cheltenham to Bournemouth on 21st August 1960. All these excursions were run by British Railways. The

success of these trains and the ease with which they rode over the Mendips perhaps shows how differently the S&D could have been run if modernisation had been attempted over the route.

Diversions

The next blow was the diversion away from the line of all through passenger services, which had long been the line's raison d'etre. From the 8th September 1962 all the through expresses using the line were withdrawn and diverted to run via Oxford and Basingstoke, including the famous "Pines Express".

To the surprise of many, British Railways 9F 2-10-0 number 92220 "Evening Star", the

One of Green Park's staff using a box of chalks to advertise springtime cheap day returns from the station in the early 1960s.

Geoff Ellis Archive

last steam locomotive to be built for British Railways, was specially brought in to haul the final "Pines" over the S&D on 8th September. The well known Bath photographer Ivo Peters asked Harold Morris, Bath Green Park's shedmaster, if "Evening Star" might be used to haul the final "Pines". A phone call was made to Terry Nichols, clerk to the Divisional Locomotive Engineer in Bristol, who contacted Derwyn Thomas the shed master at Cardiff Canton shed where 92220 was allocated. All was agreed and "Evening Star" was transferred to Bath Green Park on the 8th August, remaining there until 13th September.

The final northbound run of the "Pines" with "Evening Star" was made by 24 year old Branksome passed fireman Peter Smith and his even younger fireman Aubrey Punter. As

Peter recorded in his 1972 book "Mendips Engineman", at 426 tons the load taken over the Mendips on that day was a record for an unassisted locomotive and demonstrated the 9F's mastery over the line. On the footplate for the southbound run were driver Peter Guy and fireman Ron Hyde, also from Branksome shed, who were also responsible for taking the first "Pines" over its new route via Southampton, Basingstoke and Oxford on the following Monday morning. For the record, their locomotive on that day was West Country Class 34043 "Combe Martin", reportedly not in the best of health for an express turn. "Combe Martin" had been one of the Bulleid pacifics which was allocated to Bath back in the 1950s and had a further claim to fame over the line as in 1952 it was filmed crossing Midford viaduct for the opening scene of the Ealing comedy "The Titfield Thunderbolt". It was also the first of its class to be withdrawn from service in June 1963 due to a cracked cylinder block.

In December 1962 "Railway World" magazine featured an article headed "Last Act Begins on the Somerset & Dorset". It included a picture of "Evening Star" on the up working leaving Blandford Forum with driver Peter Smith waving to the photographer. The editor of the magazine, Geoffrey Freeman Allen, wrote in the text, *The diversion of the "Pines Express" from the Somerset & Dorset line at the end of last summer's service is generally regarded as a prelude to proposals for closure of at least part of the route.* In addition, the front cover of the magazine carried a photograph taken by Ivo Peters of the last down service running through Midsomer Norton station, with people waving from the platform and fireman Ron Hyde leaning out of the cab window. Behind the locomotive were two Eastern Region Gresley coaches and heads could be seen hanging out of

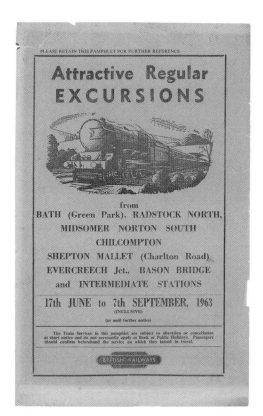

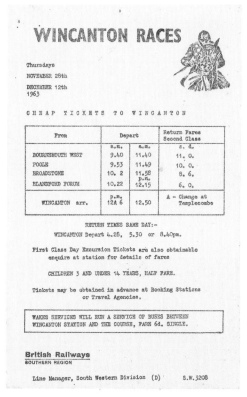

carriage windows along the train's length. 92220 was carrying a headboard on the top smokebox lamp iron, whilst on its buffer beam it carried an express lamp headcode with the train reporting code 1O95 on a disc in the centre. Its 86C Cardiff Canton shed code plate was replaced by a 82F Bath Green Park plate for the duration of its short stay on the S&D, before it was transferred back to South Wales but this time to Cardiff East Dock shed, 88A.

Disjointed Management

After the loss of the through services the line's timetable was not altered and many services continued to run to provide connections with non-existent trains. To add insult to injury, in

the following year the 9Fs reappeared (unbelievably including "Evening Star"), despite the removal of through trains and holiday expresses. This was hardly the sort of thinking espoused by the Beeching report published at the beginning of the same year.

And yet during the summer of 1963 the Western Region was also actively promoting "Attractive Regular Excursions" from "17th June to 7th September inclusive". These were available from S&D stations to locations such as Poole, Bournemouth, Weston super Mare and London Waterloo. The publicity leaflets stated that further information could be obtained from Mr D S Hart, the Divisional Manager at Temple Meads, the same individual responsible for administering the rundown of the S&D - perhaps the publicity department at London Paddington hadn't been told? Money was still being spent on promoting the S&D as late as 1965 when further posters and leaflets announcing cut price fares from various stations were printed, appearing under the auspices of the newly renamed British Rail.

Technically one long distance through passenger train did operate on the S&D right up to November 1965, as a service from London Waterloo to Weymouth still saw three coaches being detached at Bournemouth, which then formed the 11.41am service to Bath Green Park. I doubt if this connection was shown in the public timetable or that anyone ever used it as a through train from London to Bath.

In 1964 a number of freight services were withdrawn, including the diversion of the Avonmouth to Blandford fertiliser trains. From September 7th all night time freight workings were withdrawn from the line, including the 2.40am mail train from Bath to Bournemouth, necessitating the use of road transport for mails beyond Bath.

And as was often the case at this period, railway management used questionable means to show that passenger numbers were low. As an example on the S&D they conducted surveys and passenger counts in school holiday periods when it was well known that many school children used the line extensively, even if only for short journeys.

As the S&D went into its last full year of operation in 1965, an air of tired neglect settled over the whole of the system. Locomotives looked increasingly unkempt, while disused sidings lay rusting or were lifted. Some stations lost their staff and signal boxes were closed or switched out of operation when traffic was light, the boxes at Cole and Chilcompton being demolished.

However the staff still did a professional job of keeping things going, although increasingly the odds were mounting against them.

As early as December 1962 the Branch Line Re-invigoration Society had published an exhaustively researched and comprehensive report on the possibilities for improvement. All was to fall on deaf ears however and feelings ran very high. To give just one example, Templecombe based driver Den Norris was a very vocal critic of the decision to close the line he had worked on for 42 years. A Justice of the Peace and well respected member of the community, he gave up both his seat on the Parish Council and secretaryship of the local branch of the Labour Party in protest at the closure.

Remaining through services

There were a number of trains that still used the S&D as a through route after 1962, with the first being on 27th April 1963. This was an eleven coach football special, double headed as far as Bath by BR Standard 4MT 75007 and Bulleid Pacific 34067 "Tangmere" (now preserved). This train was taking Southampton fans to an FA Cup semi final game in Birmingham, which they lost 1-0 to Manchester United in front of a crowd of 68,000 at Villa Park. 75007 was again employed in 1964 to be the pilot locomotive on special workings, firstly on July the 16th with 34079 "141 Squadron" on a Cole to Coventry school special and then four days later it piloted Bulleid Pacific 34029 "Lundy" on a Christchurch to Bath and return school special.

Bank Holidays still saw additional excursions being operated to Bournemouth from both Bristol Temple Meads and Bath Green Park. The 1963 August Holiday Monday saw BR Standard 5MT 73047 in charge from Bath of a service which originated from

Bristol. It was followed south by classmate 73054 on a 10 coach train, this time starting from Bath. These workings continued in the following year, when on Whit Monday Class 8F 48660 provided assistance over the Mendips to 73049 on another excursion to the South Coast. A year later on the 1965 Whitsun Holiday Monday, two excursions were run. BR Standard 4MTs 75009 and 75054 were at the head of the train from Bristol, whilst 5MT 73051 had charge of one originating from Bath. The final Bank Holiday excursions to operate over the S&D to Bournemouth did so on August 30th 1965. Standard 5MT 73068 on a 10 coach train starting from Bristol, was piloted by the shortly to be withdrawn 4MT tank 80059 from Bath to Evercreech Junction. Meanwhile 5MT 73001 had charge of an eight coach excursion commencing at Bath. Although closure was by now not far away, these trains still saw excellent patronage.

"Foreign" Motive Power

Bath Green Park still attracted some interesting locomotive types in this period, both steam and diesel. On February 12th 1964 B1 Class 4-6-0 61143 worked into the City over the Midland route. The 5.10pm from Bristol Temple Meads to Green Park provided a variety of motive power, on May 11th Hymek D7050 was in charge, while on the next day it was formed of a DMU and then on August 14th, Warship Class D809 "Champion" worked the service. Earlier that year on Monday 18th May, Bristol Barrow Road shed allocated Jubilee Class 45682 "Trafalgar" failed at Weston near Bath, on an empty stock working from Bristol Carriage Sidings to Green Park. It suffered a fractured cylinder and after the stricken locomotive had been recovered to Bath, it was turned and placed inside the shed as though ready to work

Templecombe based 4MT 75072 has just passed over the A37 and is about to cross Charlton Road viaduct, as it drops down the grade towards Shepton Mallet station with a local service in 1961.

"Evening Star" stands on Bath shed in
September of 1962. It had been specially
transferred from Cardiff Canton to haul the final
"Pines Express".

Fireman Ron Hyde looks out of the cab as "Evening Star" comes thundering through Midsomer Norton on the final southbound run of the "Pines".

Ivo Peters, courtesy Julian Peters.

On the 10th August 1964 Radstock's 47506 has come up to Binegar to attach a van to an up train. Here it waits in the yard as 73068 passes with the 3.35pm semi fast Bristol to Bournemouth service.

Tim Chapman

Jinty 47506 has pulled the van out of the yard and then propelled it through the crossover, attaching it to the 4.15pm local from Templecombe to Bath headed by 4MT tank 80067.

Tim Chapman.

another train. Withdrawn from service in June, the locomotive remained at Bath until 15th October when it was finally removed to a scrapyard in Swansea. I can still recall seeing it cold and neglected in the dim light at the back of the S&D shed, and I often wondered what would happen to it. The diversity of motive power continued into 1965 as on 1st May Manchester based Britannia Class 70034 "Thomas Hardy" arrived on a down parcels train, on the same day that West Country 34046 "Braunton" had worked up from Bournemouth, deputising for a failed Class 4. The Brittania was an exotic visitor, and no doubt delighted the enthusiasts present on the day, but although Bulleid pacifics were also rare by this date, the same locomotive had worked up from Bournemouth two weeks previously on the 19th April, again deputising for a failed Class 4. With just weeks remaining of Western Region steam, on November 3rd an unidentified Pannier Tank put in a surprise appearance on an evening passenger working from Bristol, and for the following two evenings Gloucester based Prairie Tank 6141 was on the same service.

There was a further appearance of a Bullied Pacific on 6th November 1965 when 34044 "Woolacombe" was in charge of the 09.37am Bournemouth to Bath service, substituting for another failure of the booked motive power at Bournemouth. It returned south on the 7.55pm from Bath having spent the day on shed. This was the last recorded return working of a modified Bulleid pacific on a timetabled passenger working over the S&D before closure, although an unidentified unrebuilt pacific did apparently reach Green Park from the south on the 14th December, returning with the 3.20pm from Bath. Another member of a class once common on the S&D also made an appearance at Green Park on the previous day. Preston based Black

5 44958 worked in on a freight from Gloucester, the final time that a member of this class would visit Bath.

Large Prairie Tank 6113 from Gloucester Horton Road Shed was in theory allocated to Bath Green Park from the 2nd until the 17th of November of 1964 before being transferred back to Gloucester, although I have not found any evidence to show that it actually arrived. The reasoning that there might have been a locomotive shortage at Bath is supported to some extent by the fact that on November 17th a Hawksworth Pannier Tank 8436 was transferred from Old Oak Common shed in London to Bath, followed by classmate 8486 on March 3rd 1965. These powerful locomotives, which had been used for hauling empty coaching stock in and out of Paddington station, were being replaced by diesels and further work was no doubt being sought for them. Their presence at Bath was fairly short lived as both locomotives were withdrawn from service on June 14th 1965, being replaced by BR Standard 4MT 80059 from Bristol Barrow Road and Pannier tank 3677 from Gloucester Horton Road. After standing on the scrap siding at Bath for some weeks, both 8436 and 8486 were towed away to be cut up at Thomas Ward's yard at Britton Ferry in South Wales. Despite a very short stay, these locos were certainly used for shunting at Bath particularly at the Gas Works sidings, although no evidence has been found that they worked any trains over the S&D line. 3677 was transferred away from Bath to Oxford in September that year, while 80059 only lasted until 18th November when it was withdrawn and sent for scrap to Buttigiegs yard at Newport.

"Home" Motive Power

In August of 1965 Bath Green Park allocated BR Standard Class 5 locomotives 73015,

53807 approaches Masbury Summit with the 11.00am goods to Evercreech Junction on Saturday 5th September 1964. This was the locomotive's last day in service. Ivo Peters, courtesy Julian Peters

73051 and 73054 were all withdrawn from service. Two of these locomotives, 73015 and 73054, were only eleven years old whilst 73051 had clocked up thirteen years, based at Bath for the whole of its working existence. There would have been a lot more life left in these three locomotives and I have been told by several ex S&D footplate staff that 73054 in particular was an excellent locomotive to work on, being a fine performer and the favourite of several enginemen at Bath. The trio were taken up to the closed Gloucester Barnwood shed en route to the scrap yard, and made their final journey from there to South Wales via Chepstow on 13th October towed by 26 year old 7816 "Frilsham

Manor" from Horton Road shed. Incidentally, "Frilsham Manor" had at 11.00am on that same day been the last locomotive to leave Didcot shed under steam before it closed, transferring across to Gloucester Horton Road shed - the event making front page news on the "Didcot Advertiser" on the following Thursday. The Standard Class 5s were all subsequently cut up at John Cashmore's yard in Newport Docks later that year.

During this last full year of operation over the S&D, several incidents of note occurred with remaining BR Standard 5 locomotive 73001. Whilst working a Bath to Bournemouth service near Blandford the

On 8th March 1964 9F 92209 waits for departure in Blandford station at the head of the "The South Western Rambler" while photographers record the scene for posterity.

locomotive (according to its speedometer) reached a speed of 98mph, driver Lou Long and fireman Mike Baker were on the footplate. I would imagine it was quite a rough ride and certainly well in excess of the permitted line speed - perhaps the crew would have given the excuse that the speedometer was not reading correctly if challenged? On 1st December the same locomotive suffered a serious blow back through the fire box at Midsomer Norton station whilst working the 9.50am down train from Bath to Bournemouth. Driver Ray Stokes

was at the regulator and was accompanied on the footplate by the well known photographer Ivo Peters and a traction inspector. Miraculously they managed to avoid any serious injury, although fireman Robin Gould did suffer some slight scalding but was able to continue with his duties. 73001 was replaced by Bath 8F 48760, which was shunting at the nearby Norton Hill colliery and this took the train on as far as Templecombe, the service now running over an hour late. Surprisingly 73001 was not withdrawn from service following this

mishap, which was due to the steam pipe to the blower having fractured, but was instead repaired and returned to traffic for just four more weeks of use.

With the S&D 7Fs coming to the end of their lives, a Stanier 8F had been trialled over the S&D in May 1961 when 48450 from Bristol's St Philips Marsh shed worked a freight from Bath to Evercreech Junction and return. The test was successful, unsurprisingly as these locomotives had worked over the line in the War. 53807 was the last 7F in service, and was withdrawn on 5th September 1964 after working the 11.00am Bath to Evercreech Junction goods and returning light engine and brake van, the crew for this last run being Driver David Massey and Fireman Beverly Reynolds.

48436 and 48471 were transferred from St Philips Marsh shed in October of 1961, and further allocations and changes followed over the next few years as the 7Fs were progressively withdrawn from service. In June 1965 the final transfers took place when 48706 and 48760 arrived from Llanelly shed, just before it closed. It had been intended that these locomotives would be placed in store, but in the event they were both pressed into use and alongside 48309 they were the only 8Fs still operating at the end of the S&D.

A class of locomotive that put in a late appearance at Bath and over the S&D was the Standard Class 4MT tank. They first appeared on the 4th November 1963, being provided for use over the line by the Southern Region. These versatile engines were then increasingly used and served the line very well in its closing years.

A few diesels

Peak diesels started working in and out of Green Park fairly regularly in later years. In 1964 one even banked the Writhlington coal empties up from Bath to Combe Down tunnel, the only time a member of this class ran on the S&D. On the 13th October of the same year, Laira based North British D6320 worked over the branch from Highbridge, running at least as far as Evercreech Junction and hauling a Western inspection saloon. This was followed by a similar working in the spring of 1965, when Hymek D7024 from Bristol's Bath Road depot worked an inspection saloon over the southern end of the line. It was carrying a local MP (believed to be North Dorset constituency Conservative MP

Sir Richard Glyn) who was assessing what hardship would be caused to constituents if the S&D closed.

Non passenger workings

Over this period there were still a handful of non passenger workings which went beyond local destinations. One such service which operated to the very end was the "perishables" to Derby, which was scheduled to depart from Templecombe at 8.25pm and was often worked by Green Park based guard Bernard Ware.

Bernard made notes of several trips and on December 16th 1965 he recorded a fourteen minute "over run" at Shepton Mallet, where an extra van full of Post Office parcels was added to the train. BR Standard 4MT Tank 80039 was in charge on Wednesday 29th December with a load of eight vans and at Evercreech Junction two further vans were attached, destined for Newcastle. These extras had been worked down the branch from Glastonbury carrying shoes from the Clarks factory in Street. Ten vans from Evercreech over the Mendips was quite a load for a Standard Tank

Day Tickets

from **Ashcott**—Second class fares

	s d		s d
Bournemouth	12 0	Highbridge for B.-on-S.	2 8
Glastonbury & S.	1 1	Poole	11 6

from **Bason Bridge**—Second class fares

Bournemouth	13 6	Highbridge for B.-on.S.	10
Glastonbury & S.	3 3	Poole	12 6

from **Binegar**— Second class fares

Bath Green Park	4 9	Poole	10 9
Bournemouth	11 6	Shepton Mallet	1 10
Glastonbury & S.	5 0	Waterloo	36 3
Highbridge for B.-on.S.	8 3		

from **Bitton**—Second class fares

Bath Green Park	2 2	Bristol T.M.	2 5

from **Chilcompton**—Second class fares

Bath Green Park	4 3	Poole	11 0
Bournemouth	11 6	Shepton Mallet	2 11
Glastonbury & S.	5 9	Waterloo	35 6
Highbridge for B.-on-S.	9 0		

from **Edington Burtle**—Second class fares

Bournemouth	13 0	Highbridge for B.-on-S.	1 10
Glastonbury & S.	2 7	Poole	11 6

from **Evercreech Junction**—Second class fares

Bath Green Park	7 6	Poole	9 9
Bournemouth	10 6	Waterloo	33 6
Highbridge for B.-on-S.	5 9	Wincanton	2 10

from **Evercreech New**—Second class fares

Bath Green Park	7 0	Poole	9 9
Bournemouth	10 6	Waterloo	34 0
Highbridge for B.-on-S.	6 0		

from **Fishponds**—Second class fares

Bath Green Park	3 3	Mangotsfield	1 1
Bristol T.M.	1 1	Weston-s.-Mare	6 6

from **Glastonbury & S.**—Second class fares

Bournemouth	11 6	Waterloo	36 6
Highbridge for B.-on-S.	3 3	Weston-s.-Mare	6 0
Poole	10 9	West Pennard	2 2

from **Mangotsfield**—Second class fares

Bath Green Park	2 11	Bristol T.M.	1 9

from **Masbury Halt**—Second class fare

Bath Green Park	5 3

from **Midford**—Second class fares

Bath Green Park	1 7	Highbridge for B.-on-S.	12 0
Bournemouth	14 6	Poole	13 0
Glastonbury & S.	9 0		

from **Midsomer Norton**—Second class fares

	s d		s d
Bath Green Park	3 9	Poole	11 6
Bournemouth	12 6	Shepton Mallet	3 3
Glastonbury & S.	7 0	Waterloo	37 3
Highbridge for B.-on-S.	9 6		

from **Oldland Common**—Second class fares

Bath Green Park	2 5	Fishponds	1 10
Bristol T.M.	1 1		

from **Pylle Halt**—Second class fares

Bournemouth	10 6	Highbridge for B.-on-S.	5 6
Glastonbury & S.	2 9	Poole	9 9

from **Radstock**—Second class fares

Bath Green Park	3 0	Poole	11 6
Bournemouth	12 6	Shepton Mallet	3 9
Glastonbury & S.	7 6	Waterloo	37 3
Highbridge for B.-on-S.	11 0		

from **Shapwick**—Second class fares

Bournemouth	12 3	Highbridge for B.-on-S.	2 2
Glastonbury & S.	1 10	Poole	11 6

from **Shepton Mallet**—Second class fares

Bath Green Park	5 9	Poole	10 6
Bournemouth	11 0	Waterloo	34 9
Glastonbury & S.	4 3	Wincanton	3 9
Highbridge for B.-on-S.	7 6		

from **Shoscombe & S. Hill Halt**— Second class fares

Bath Green Park	2 6	Highbridge for B.-on-S.	10 6
Glastonbury & S.	8 0		

from **Staple Hill**—Second class fares

Bath Green Park	3 3	Oldland Common	1 7
Bitton	1 10	Warmley	1 1
Bristol T.M.	1 4	Weston-s.-Mare	6 9
Mangotsfield	10		

from **Warmley**—Second class fares

Bath Green Park	2 8	Fishponds	1 7
Bristol T.M.	2 5		

from **Wellow**—Second class fares

Bath Green Park	2 2	Highbridge for B.-on-S.	11 0
Bournemouth	13 6	Poole	12 6
Glastonbury & S.	8 6		

from **West Pennard**—Second class fares

Bournemouth	10 3	Poole	9 9
Glastonbury	2 2	Waterloo	35 0
Highbridge for B.-on-S.	5 0	Weston-s.-Mare	7 0

From 1 February, 1965 and until further notice
Daily by any train (service permitting). Back by any train the same day.
First class tickets (when available) are approximately 50% higher.
Children 3 and under 14 years, half-fare.
British Rail Western Region

On the 2nd May 1965 the "Wessex Downsman" runs in to Bath behind 4F 44264, passing 8F 48309 which would take the tour on over the S&D. In the background can be seen Bath gasworks and the extensive premises of Stothert and Pitt.

Ivo Peters, courtesy Julian Peters.

Fireman Ian Bunnet takes a breather as 48309
lifts the "Wessex Downsman" out of Bath. In a
few moments the train will have plunged into the
choking confines of Devonshire Tunnel.

Alan Chandler, courtesy ColourRail.

unassisted, but on the following evening sister locomotive 80037 had an even heavier load, leaving Templecombe with nine vans with a further two attached at Evercreech Junction, this time destined for Crewe and Newcastle. The very last run of the "perishables" took place on Friday 31st December. This train had the same loading of 9 vans plus two added at Evercreech and was behind Standard 4MT Tank 80043. It is quite clear from these observations that despite the rundown of the line, there was still significant traffic being carried over the S&D to the very end.

Special Trains

With the threat of closure clearly hanging over the S&D, a number of rail tours were organised which even at this late stage brought unusual motive power to the line.

On the 8th March 1964 The Southern Counties Touring Society organised "The South Western Rambler Rail Tour" which originated from London Waterloo station. The two principle locomotives used during the day were Britannia Class 70020 "Mercury" and Class 9F 2-10-0 number 92209. At Salisbury station the 9F took over, running down the former Southern main line to Templecombe where Pannier 4634 was attached to the rear, hauling the train back down to Number Two Junction allowing the 9F to continue its run south. Blandford was reached ten minutes early providing the tour participants ample time to obtain photo-

graphs, before setting off for Bournemouth Central at 3.30pm, where 70020 "Mercury" rejoined the train for the run back to Waterloo. It is unclear if 92209 used the S&D to return to its home shed at Newport Ebbw Junction, although this would have been the most direct route.

A notable tour was the Home Counties Railway Society's "Somerset and Dorset" on the 7th June, originating at Waterloo and hauled to Bournemouth Central by 35002 "Union Castle". From there two ex S&D types 4F 44558 and 7F 53807 double headed the train to Bath, including a trip along the branch to Highbridge and back. At Bath, 7023

On 30th August 1965 chime whistle fitted Standard 73001 stands at Shillingstone, waiting to cross an up working. It was working the last Bank Holiday special from Bath to Bournemouth.   Richard Clayton

Richard Clayton was travelling on the excursion and photographed driver Ben Ford and his young fireman John Sawyer before getting back on to the train.   Richard Clayton.

In late summer 1965 withdrawn Hawksworth
Panniers 8486 and 8436 stand on the scrap line in
Bath in front of an unidentified 8F.

The guard surveys his train on a dismal Saturday
2nd October 1965 at Green Park station. Headed
by 4MT 80067 and consisting of three Southern
Region coaches, it would shortly be departing for
Templecombe.   Peter Barnfield.

On Saturday 10th July 1965 a Post Office worker
at Highbridge takes a well loaded trolley of mail
from an S&D arrival across to the Great Western
Station, assisted by members of the station staff.

Peter Barnfield.

At just after 10.00pm on Saturday 1st January 1966, the crew of the 7.05pm from Bath pose for the photographer at Poole station. This was the last down train to run over the whole length of the S&D under the normal timetable, starting from Bristol at 5.55pm.   Tim Chapman

"Penrice Castle" took over for the next leg to Gloucester, from where 7025 "Sudely Castle" took the tour back to Paddington. This working saw the last pairing of two S&D types on a train and probably the first visit of a Western "Castle" to Green Park.

The initial tour of the following year was on 28th March 1965 when the Southern Counties Touring Society again organised a charter. This was "The Southern Wanderer" originating from London Victoria station using BR Standard 5MT 73022 from Eastleigh shed, which worked the seven coach train west via Bournemouth, Poole and Broadstone and then up over the S&D to Templecombe Number Two Junction. As the loco was not fitted with a single line tablet catcher, token exchanges had to be carried out manually, but the locomotive still put in a good performance arriving at Templecombe five minutes ahead of its booked time. At Number Two Junction (the train did not go up into the station) the Standard gave way to 4F 44560, an ex S&D locomotive. This was specially brought in from Gloucester shed to take the charter to Evercreech Junction and then along the Branch to Highbridge and return. It continued to Templecombe station, where 35023 "Holland Afrika Line" was waiting to make a fast run back to London. The Merchant Navy had earlier made history when it ran light from Broadstone to Templecombe. Special dispensation had been given for this movement, as the class were officially banned from the S&D owing to their weight and axle loading.

The following week on 4th April the Locomotive Club of Great Britain's "The Wessex Downsman Number 1" set off from London Waterloo behind S15 4-6-0 30837 to Reading, where Hall Class 6963 "Throwley Hall" took the train forward to Bristol Temple Meads via the Devizes line, which also closed in 1966. At Bristol Temple Meads 4F 44466 took over for the run to Bath Green Park, piloted as far as Mangotsfield by Hymek D7007 owing to its 10 coaches. The train suffered from late running and was seventy minutes behind time when it left Bath for Bournemouth West behind 8F 48309. This was to be further compounded over the S&D as the 8F was not steaming well, taking seventy minutes to travel the twenty two miles from Bath to Shepton Mallet. By the time the train left Bournemouth West behind Battle of Britain Class 34051 "Winston Churchill", the deficit had been reduced to 61 minutes, but further slow running saw the train arriving back in the Capital some 83 minutes late.

The popularity of this special saw a repeat being operated on 2nd May as "The Wessex Downsman Number 2". This tour took the identical route but used 4F 44264, although as the load had been reduced to eight coaches there was no need for a diesel pilot from Bristol. Timekeeping on this train was much better, arriving at Bath just 15 minutes late. With 48309 at the head once again departure from Green Park was 23 minutes late, but the 8F performed well this time in the hands of driver John Stamp and fireman Ian Bunnett, arriving at Bournemouth West just 18 minutes adrift. 34051 "Winston Churchill" also put in a "spirited" run to Waterloo further reducing the final deficit to just 5 minutes.

On the 12th June, 92238 from Gloucester Horton Road shed became the last Class 9F to work over the S&D. This was on the Warwickshire Railway Society's "Somerset & Dorset Joint and Eastleigh Tour", which originated at Birmingham Snow Hill station and was brought south to Bath by Black 5 44777 from Saltley shed. This was the final time that a Black 5 would be seen working into Green Park on a passenger train, albeit a rail tour. Unfortunately, and despite being only eight years old, the 9F was in poor health and already leaking copious amounts of steam before the tour had left Bath. The run over the S&D was in trouble from the moment the train left, with speed down to a snail's pace at times, putting it far behind schedule. Driver Ray Adams and fireman Ian Bunnett from Bath shed also had to contend with a crowded footplate, as an inspector and a member of the tour organising committee were on board, allowing little room to fire the ailing locomotive. At Binegar the loco had to stop for a "blow up" before continuing its crawl over the Mendip Hills, which were covered in thick mist on the day. It was later reported that part of the problem was caused by a cylinder cover blowing off the locomotive. Whatever the reason the run achieved a measure of fame for the locomotive, as a photograph of it crawling along was used on the cover of Peter Hansford's recording "Trains in Trouble" - although little of the engine can be seen as it is enveloped in steam. Eventually reaching Bournemouth considerably behind time, the train was taken forward to Eastleigh by 34097 "Holsworthy". 92238 was turned before making its way back light engine over the S&D to Bath and then to its home shed at Gloucester. The loco was withdrawn from service just two months later from Severn Tunnel Junction shed and was scrapped at Cashmores of Newport in December 1965. Although this marked the last run of a 9F over the S&D, it was not the final appearance of the class at Green Park as we shall see later.

Whilst engines were being brought in to haul railtours over the S&D, one of Bath's engines was sent away to head a railtour on 12th December 1965. Class 8F 48309 was sent light engine to Oxford, where it took over a leg of the LCGB's "The Cross Countryman". The tour had originated at London Waterloo and arrived at Oxford twenty minutes late behind 34015 "Exmouth". 48309 was used for the section to Bedford St. Johns and return, but unfortunately this part of the tour was beset with slow running due to signal checks and single line working, and arrival back at the University City was some 82 minutes late. Here 34015 "Exmouth" replaced 48309, which after being serviced at the shed made the long trip back to Bath.

Films and a Song

Over this period the S&D made some brief appearances in popular culture. Two of its stations, Blandford Forum and Midsomer Norton, were mentioned in Flanders and Swann's famous song "Slow Train", written in July 1963 to lament the impending loss of country stations under the Beeching Report. On the 29th March of the same year the BBC transmitted Brian Johnson's superb "Let's Imagine A Branch Line Railway", in which John Betjeman was memorably filmed travelling over the branch from Evercreech to Highbridge and Burnham on Sea, documenting the journey and landscape with his characteristic poignancy and wit. This filming had taken place the previous summer.

In September 1965, Bath shed's "Jinty" 47276 took a starring role in the railway scenes of the comedy film "The Wrong Box", which featured Green Park masquerading as a London terminus alongside a number of other locations in Bath. The studio's art department carried out some minor alterations to the locomotive by removing its 82F shed code plate and giving it a smokebox number of 727, achieved by painting out the first and last digits of its number plate. It was also painted light green on the fireman's side only, but retained a black smokebox. The locomotive sported its unusual colour scheme until its withdrawal from service in March 1966 and eventual scrapping. This film, which went on general release in 1966, starred a large number of well known actors of the time, including John Mills, Peter Cook, Dudley Moore, Michael Caine and Nanette Newman.

And all that Jazz

Going back a little, on the 30th April 1961 Bernard Ware, a porter at the time, recorded in his notes that whilst working the 2.00 to

On the 4th April 1965, three friends pose in Lyncombe Vale, having just recorded the "Wessex Downsman" slogging through into Combe Down Tunnel.   Richard Clayton.

10.00pm shift at Green Park he had posed for publicity photographs with a jazz band. This turned out to be for a fringe event to the Bath International Music Festival, which took place on Friday 9th June and featured a Bristol based DMU running a shuttle service between Green Park and Wellow stations. Making a number of runs during the night, the event was billed as the "11 o'clock Special" and the DMU operated, as the title implied, from 11.00pm. At Green Park station Humphrey Lyttelton and his band performed on a specially built stage, erected from the concourse over the two centre tracks, while free food was provided from two restaurant coaches parked in the south platform. (This was a tickets only event). The "Titfield Thunderbolt" was shown in a waiting room at Green Park and at Wellow a pig roast was

Robert and Patricia Coles pose for the Bath Chronicle's photographer at the end of Green Park's arrival platform on 9th June 1961, the night of the 11 o'clock Special.

Robert Coles and Geoff Ellis Archive.

"Pearce Cadwalladers Stompers" and friends pose for a publicity shot on the tracks at Green Park station on the 30th April 1961.

Nigel Hunt.

staged as the centrepiece of a giant barbecue. The "Pearce Cadwallader Stompers", Bath's most popular band in the trad boom years, played on the train as it travelled up and down the line to Wellow. Local jazz enthusiasts Patricia and Robert Coles had their picture taken by Bath Chronicle photographer Geoff Ellis, sitting astride the buffer stops of the north platform, and the resulting photograph appeared in the paper on the following day. At the end of the event Robert, ever the gentleman, escorted Patricia back to her flat in the City. He then returned to the by now deserted station and settled down for some sleep in the ladies waiting room, from where he was shortly disturbed by what sounded like a train arriving. Going out on to the platform to investigate, he could hardly believe his eyes as he thought he saw 46100 "Royal Scot" at the head of a parcels train! This nocturnal apparition can be confirmed as Ivo Peters photographed the locomotive at Bath the next day. "Royal Scot" had arrived on a pigeon special on Friday night and then departed north with the "Pines" on Saturday afternoon. You may wonder about Robert returning to Green Park to sleep that night, but nobody challenged him, and as he says - it was the S&D and "his" railway!

On Saturday 10th June 1961, "Royal Scot" has difficulty keeping her feet as she comes off shed to take the "Pines Express" out of Bath. The locomotive had arrived very early the same day on a pigeon special from the north.

Ivo Peters, courtesy Julian Peters.

Chapter Two

THE FIRST "LAST DAY" AND THE EMERGENCY TIMETABLE

———•—◦—•———

THE ELEVENTH HOUR withdrawal of one of the bus operators in late 1965 meant that British Railways were unable to close the S&D as planned. The line would continue into the New Year, but operating a reduced "emergency timetable" using the remaining steam locomotives and stock. By the middle of February 1966 a replacement bus operator had been found and a new closure date was set for Monday 7th March. All of this was an embarrassment to the Western authorities as 3rd January was to have been the date from which steam power was eliminated from their region.

A number of specials had been arranged to travel over the line prior to its closure on 3rd January, but owing to the postponement only two actually ran. Two further tours organised by The Great Western Society and the Stephenson Locomotive Society were put back to the final weekend in March.

The Saturday tour

On 1st January the Locomotive Club of Great Britain ran the first of the tours – "The Mendip Merchantman". Providing a full restaurant car service of breakfast, lunch, afternoon tea and dinner, it set out at 8.30am from London Waterloo station behind Merchant Navy Class 35011 "General Steam Navigation". It ran via Bournemouth and Poole and then took the S&D to Templecombe Number Two Junction. This was the second visit of a Merchant Navy Class to the S&D but as the line was closing the authorities waived the earlier mentioned ban. At Templecombe Ivatt tanks 41307 and 41283 took over for the run up the main line to Evercreech Junction, where a stop was made in pouring rain before heading along the branch to Highbridge, departing just 14 minutes behind schedule. On arrival at Highbridge, the passengers all left the train while the stock was shunted from the S&D station across to the main line platforms. Here Class 9F 92243 took over for the run to Bath Green Park via Bristol Temple Meads and Mangotsfield, departing Highbridge 4 minutes early. The 9F had been sent to Bath from Barrow Road shed just prior to its closure in November especially for this railtour. From Lawrence Hill Junction to Fishponds the ten coach special was banked by D864 "Zambesi", but all was not well with 92243, as it failed completely at Warmley due to the brick arch in the firebox collapsing. Waiting at Bath to take the special back over the S&D to Templecombe were 8Fs 48760 and 48309. When the plight of 92243 became known, 48760 was hastily uncoupled and sent to Warmley to pull the stricken engine and train to Bath, eventually arriving 89 nine

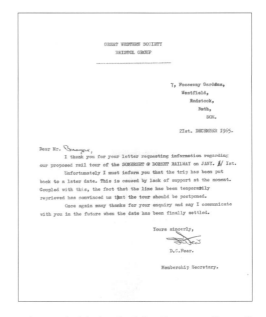

minutes behind schedule. I can well recall standing on the "tump" opposite Green Park shed watching all these happenings on this cold day. I pitied the passengers who had suffered from Highbridge to Bath, as neither the 9F or 48760 were fitted for steam heating. The journey onwards over the Mendips would have been better, as 48309 was fitted with steam heat, being one of only two 8F's so fitted for Royal Train duties back in 1955. Upon arrival at Templecombe "General

**35011 "General Steam Navigation" heads the
LCGB's "Mendip Merchantman" northwards near
Stalbridge on the morning of 1st January.**
Trevor Owen, courtesy ColourRail

At Glastonbury, passengers have descended en masse from the "Mendip Merchantman" to photograph Ivatt tanks 41283 and 41307. The locomotives moved forwards after this picture was taken to clear the two wagons that were obstructing the photographers view. Brilliant sunshine had by now replaced the rain and gloom encountered earlier in the day.

Tim Chapman

The two Ivatt tanks get the "Mendip Merchantman" under way for Highbridge following the stop at Glastonbury.

Alan Chandler, courtesy ColourRail.

Steam Navigation" took over again for the run back to London, having been serviced in the shed, the train eventually arriving at Waterloo 76 minutes late.

Service train problems

On the same day resident S&D Standard Class 4s 75072 and 75073 both suffered problems on their service trains. 75072 worked the 11.45am Bournemouth to Bath, but was in a poor state of health and had to stop for a lengthy "blow up" at Evercreech Junction before eventually departing some 30 minutes late, thereby delaying the branch train to Highbridge hauled by Ivatt tank 41290. Despite the closure reprieve this branch service, comprising just one Mk1 type Brake Composite coach and a van, was packed to capacity with enthusiasts. Even more passengers were jammed in for the 2.18pm return working back to Evercreech behind classmate 41296, which put in a lively performance for those on board. Meanwhile 75072 had been forced to make a longer stop at Shepton Mallet to raise steam again before proceeding to Bath. This loco had recently been running well, having worked off the S&D on a Bournemouth to Newcastle express throughout to Oxford via Basingstoke in the previous month. 75073 suffered similar problems on the 4.15pm Templecombe to Bath and these two troubled workings were to be the last runs for these locomotives. On arrival back at Bath shed they were both turned before having their fires dropped for the last time and being taken out of service - although according to official records they had both had been withdrawn on the previous day.

The Sunday Tour

35011 "General Steam Navigation" was used again on Sunday the 2nd for the RCTS

The Reverend John Sutters only had a basic camera and couldn't afford a lot of film, so one has to admire him for taking this effective shot through a hailstorm. 9F 92243 is just crossing over from the down to the up line as it gets the "Mendip Merchantman" away from Highbridge towards Bristol.

Rev. John Sutters, courtesy Phil Sutters.

"Somerset and Dorset Rail Tour" which departed from Waterloo at 8.30am. The Merchant Navy headed the train via Bournemouth and Poole to Broadstone Junction, where U Class 2-6-0 31639 and West Country Class 34015 "Exmouth" took the train over the S&D to Bath, stopping en route at Evercreech Junction for water. Broadstone platform was reported to be very icy and several passengers are said to have "gone flying" as they rushed around getting their photographs. The U was a rare visitor to the line although two members of the class, 31621 and 31906, had been unsuccessfully trialled over the S&D back in March 1954. On arrival at Bath 8F 48309 backed on to the ten coach special, from where it ran to Highbridge via Mangotsfield and Bristol Temple Meads. At Highbridge Ivatt tanks

41283 and 41307 took over for a trip over the Levels to Evercreech Junction and then to Templecombe. 35011 took the train on to London, having earlier run light from Broadstone. This tour carried 480 passengers and had been oversubscribed by 120.

The New Year

The emergency timetable came into force on the following day and saw a substantial reduction in the number of services being operated over the S&D, with the main line effectively being "cut in two". There were just four trains each way between Bath and Templecombe, although the southern section between Bournemouth and Templecombe had one extra. Through journeys were now next to impossible, the best connection in the down direction being the 6.45am from Bath which reached Templecombe at 8.29am, where the intending through passenger faced a wait of just over half an hour for the 9.05am service to Bournemouth. This train actually terminated at Branksome, where a further change would be required for travel to Bournemouth proper. The other three down services gave impossibly long waits for through passengers. The up direction fared slightly better as the 6.46pm off Bournemouth was in fact a through train to Bath, arriving at 9.50pm, but none of the other up services offered a connection. It is interesting that on the southern section of the line the 1.25pm up service started from Branksome rather than Bournemouth and actually operated beyond Templecombe to Evercreech Junction. This however only after a wait of 48 minutes at Templecombe, eventually arriving at Evercreech at 3.58pm. The locomotive was normally turned at the shed before the train returned south at 4.13pm to Bournemouth. On Mondays to Fridays there was a 3.37pm all stations service from Bournemouth which terminated at Sturminster Newton. It is understood that this service was primarily for school traffic as on Saturdays it departed 6 minutes later from Bournemouth and only ran as far as Blandford. On weekdays and Saturdays the train would return empty to Bailey Gate to form a 6.32pm service back to Bournemouth, so that the milk traffic from the busy dairy could be accommodated. There were just two services in each direction on the branch, the first left Highbridge at 6.55am and ran through to Templecombe, but did not call at Cole or Wincanton. The 4.00pm from Highbridge only operated to Evercreech Junction, but still picked up extensive parcels traffic from the Clarks factory at Glastonbury for onward transit to London. In the other direction, the 8.20am from Templecombe operated through to Highbridge, with the

afternoon working starting from Evercreech Junction at 5.15pm. On the Midland line to Bath services were diesel hauled, with a diagram starting from Bristol and providing three round trips on weekdays and two on Saturdays. The last departure at 1.00pm from Bath on a Saturday certainly didn't provide a good service for anyone wanting to do weekend shopping in Bath or Bristol.

Temporary improvements

The Western Region had defended the use of the "emergency timetable" but were nonetheless embarrassed by the situation, being forced to explain that they did not have the resources and staff to operate a more effective timetable. There were many complaints and from the 15th January British Rail announced that they would provide an additional emergency bus service from Shoscombe and Wellow to Bath, and the 4.00pm departure from Highbridge and its corresponding return working would be extended from Evercreech to Templecombe. In truth the minimal service now being operated was not fit for purpose and the line struggled on in an unhappy limbo up to the final closure on Monday the 7th March.

Remaining locomotives

Lines of withdrawn motive power stood forlornly at both Bath and Templecombe sheds, leaving just a handful of run down locomotives to work the reduced services. At Bath shed just eight locomotives officially remained in traffic, these were Panniers 3681 and 3758, Jinty tanks 47276 and 47506, and 8Fs 48309, 48444, 48706 and 48760. Of these 3758 was kept in the shed with the snow plough ready in case of inclement weather, while 47276 was shedded at Radstock for shunting the coal traffic. Class 8F 48444 had earlier been placed in store but had been

returned to service to see regular use on coal trains until 14th February when it was finally withdrawn from service. The locomotives taken out of service on the 31st December at Bath shed were the passenger types, 5MTs 73001 and 73068 and the 3MT tanks 82001, 82030 and 82041, although two of these actually made their last runs on the day after their withdrawal. 73001 was in poor condition when it worked the 9.50am Bath to Bournemouth, together with a return working to Bath. It departed south some five minutes late, but arrived at Radstock only 1 minute down. Although sounding very "off beat", both Midsomer Norton and Evercreech Junction were reached on time. Green liveried BR Standard tank 82041 worked the 10.10am Bath to Bristol and back, one of the last steam hauled ordinary passenger services over the Midland line.

There were nine Ivatt tanks and four Standard 4MT tank locomotives in service at Templecombe shed from 3rd January 1966. These were more suitable to the remaining passenger operations on the line than the engines allocated to Bath. Standard 4MT tank 80039 was withdrawn from Templecombe on the 21st January followed by Ivatt 41291 in February and both were moved to Bath for storage. Ivatt tank 41223 was sent light engine to Bath on 25th February and withdrawn on the 7th March.

Bournemouth shed continued to supply locomotives during the emergency timetable, predominately to work on the southern section of the line as far as Templecombe but also for the 6.18pm through service to Bath. Bournemouth based locomotives observed on the S&D during this period included Standard 4MT moguls 76005, 76011, 76014, 76026 and 76057, plus BR Standard 4MT tanks 80013, 80035, 80085 and 80138. Locomotives from Eastleigh shed were also observed on the line,

**U class 31639 and West Country 34015
"Exmouth" on the RCTS "Somerset and Dorset
Rail Tour" pictured at Evercreech Junction
during a water stop. Sunday 2nd January.   RCTS.**

BR Standard 4MT 75076 was noted on Green Park shed on the 2nd January and is believed to have left the following day, while sister locomotive 75078 was spotted at Templecombe in the same month.

Observations and the Steam Ban

Train services on the main line during the emergency timetable were generally formed of three coach sets provided by the Southern Region, with few spare coaches now on hand to add to any of these sets if required. On the branch, the trains were formed of a single former Great Western Hawksworth coach in maroon livery plus a parcels van, or the Hawksworth with the addition of a BR brake composite coach. If passengers were lucky they would have heating in the trains, providing the system was working correctly, but if one of Bath's 8Fs happened to be allocated to a passenger working they were out of luck, as neither 48444, 48706 nor 48760 were equipped to provide steam heat.

The Bath 8Fs were normally allocated to work the loaded coal trains from Writhlington Colliery to Bath and the return empty wagons. They also worked the coal traffic onwards to Bristol West Depot, from where the coal was destined for the Portishead power station. 48706 was recorded heading a coal train to Eastville Gas Works in Bristol on 24th January. 48760 managed to travel quite a distance on 26th February when it worked an afternoon freight from Bath as far as Severn Tunnel Junction, being observed passing Patchway at 4.15pm.

Another locomotive which broke the Western's steam ban was Birmingham based 9F 92155, which hauled a freight from Gloucester into Green Park in February 1966, making it the last member of the class to work there. Sister locomotive 92243 which had failed back in January was still on the scrap

Photographers record 48309 standing at Bristol Temple Meads where it was booked for an eleven minute stop before departure for Highbridge at 2.45pm.   RCTS.

line, now with a chalked inscription "steam for ever" on its smokebox. At least Bath shed still had the facilities to service 92155 before it headed home northwards.

An intriguing sighting in this period, reported by a reliable source but which I have been unable to further confirm, was that of a Hymek diesel standing at Wincanton station one afternoon. I don't know what it was doing, maybe it was on a test for working demolition trains or carrying out an inspection in preparation for closure. The locomotive could have gained access to the S&D by various routes, but no further reports or observations of the event have so far been found.

Bath Green Park station in this period became a collection point for redundant furniture and fittings from stations such as Wellow and Chilcompton which had become unstaffed halts. This was piled up on the concourse at the end of the northern platform. During several visits I was curious to see what was there and I spent quite some time looking through desks and cabinets completely unchallenged. I found many luggage labels of GWR, Southern Railway and LMS origins along with various parcels labels, invoices and the like. I did liberate some of the labels and I still have a small number of them today, but what happened to all the artefacts and remaining paperwork piled up on the platform I do not know.

Snowfalls occurred on the 10th and 20th January which affected services over the S&D. Up to 10 inches was reported as falling on the 20th and this was further aggravated in the south by gale force winds. The snowfall did not warrant the use of snow ploughs, but it did cause delays and disruption to the already sparse service. The bad weather continued into February and on the 5th of that month there was ice and freezing fog to contend with too. The 7.00am Templecombe to Bath service was to suffer that day, when it was declared a failure by its driver between Evercreech and Shepton Mallet after stalling in the icy conditions. The Class 4MT Standard tank hauling the train was eventually coaxed by its crew to Shepton Mallet, with assistance being summoned from Templecombe shed. An Ivatt tank was despatched northwards running bunker first and arrived at Shepton Mallet to take the stricken train to Bath. However, the handful of passengers on the service had by

this time disappeared, presumably due to the cold as the Standard tank had been removed to a siding and therefore wasn't supplying steam heating to the train.

Although I attended a school in Bath, which was right beside the former Great Western main line and gave a very clear view of passing trains, my allegiance was firmly with the S&D. I had no interest at the time in the Western Region's diesel hydraulics which roared past the school, although I did pay attention when trains of withdrawn Southern Region steam locomotives were hauled past en route to South Wales scrap yards, recognising some of these as having worked over the S&D. As the closure date drew closer, I spent as much time as I could after school on the "tump" opposite Bath shed, or sometimes I would go down to

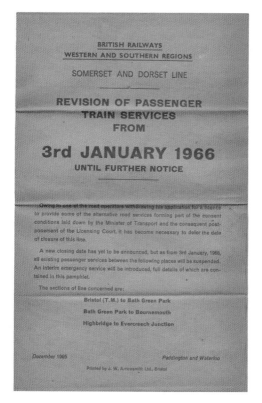

48309 stands at Highbridge after arrival from Bristol with the RCTS tour. It will shortly be shunted over to the S&D station, situated to the right and rear of the train. RCTS.

Green Park station to try to persuade a friendly driver to let me up into the cab of his locomotive. There were now fewer trains to see and I would just manage to get there to see the 2.00pm departure from Templecombe arrive at 3.40pm, which would be followed in by the 3.10pm from Bristol. This arrived behind a diesel, normally a Hymek or Peak class, at 3.47pm. After a quick run round this set off back to Bristol at 4.00pm and I would stay to see the departure of the 4.25pm to Templecombe before heading home. Since moving to Bath I had managed to "cab" quite a number of locomotives whilst they were waiting at the buffer stops at Green Park Station and would quite often get a ride to the end of the platform as the engine reversed out.

On Saturday 19th January Peter Barnfield recorded this sad scene at Bailey Gate station while waiting for an up train. Although the station was still open, all of the posters and timetable boards had been stripped ahead of closure. Peter Barnfield.

On Friday 4th March Standard mogul 76026 is pictured near Cole hauling the two withdrawn Class 4 locomotives from Bath to Templecombe. J.J. Smith, courtesy Bluebell Archive.

On rare occasions the crew would ask if I would like a footplate ride back to the sheds and this of course was never refused - even if it meant getting home late and being told off. During the emergency timetable I recorded "cabbing" 76026, 80037, 80041 and 80043 but my last ride out to the sheds was to be on the footplate of the rather filthy Standard mogul 76026. I can still remember it clearly, the engine clanking its way out of the station and then reversing back to the turntable. I climbed down from the footplate just before it went to be turned and made my way across the tracks in front of the S&D shed and along the cinder path out onto the road. There appeared to be locomotives out of use everywhere all looking in a sorry and sad condition. I had been told by the crew of 76026 to get out quickly so I wouldn't be seen. Whoever that crew were, they certainly made my day!

The Final Friday
On 4th March Bournemouth based 76026 had the poignant task of hauling two dead locomotives on the first leg of their journey to the breakers yard. Standard 4MTs 75072 and 75073, withdrawn and stored at Bath Green Park shed from the beginning of January, were being returned to their home shed at Templecombe for temporary stabling.

The forlorn looking formation left Bath just before midday and it is believed that the crew on 76026 were driver R. Williams and fireman L. Hanks. Brakesmen rode on the dead locomotives as there was no brake van attached. On arrival at Templecombe, the two locomotives were shunted into a siding by the shed to wait further movement south. 76026 then worked the 4.18pm passenger service back to Bath before spending a last night there on shed.

Ivatt tank 41290 was in use as the pilot locomotive at Templecombe while sister loco 41249 was in use on the branch service. Standard 4MT tank 80041 was used on the 2.00pm service from Templecombe to Bath with fireman Ian Bunnett working his last turn on the S&D. 80043 was recorded on a Templecombe to Bath service while 76005

On 19th February Peter called in to Wincanton
to photograph that afternoon's up service, seen
here running in to the station behind an
unidentified and unkempt Standard mogul.
A trilby wearing stationmaster has come out of
his domain to watch and a footplateman stands
to the rear. Complete with cycle clips and coat
slung across his bicycle he is presumably going
on or off duty, but for how much longer?

Peter Barnfield.

A few parcels have been unloaded, the guard is
giving right away and the box appears to be
switched out as all signals are "off". Passengers
walk down the platform towards the footbridge,
although the man in the raincoat is just watching
proceedings.   Peter Barnfield

was at the head of the 3.30pm Templecombe to Evercreech Junction and then the 4.13pm return working to Bournemouth Central. Bournemouth's 76016 together with 80085 from Feltham shed were also observed working Bournemouth to Templecombe services. Class 3F 47276 spent its last day in service shunting wagons at Writhlington Colliery sidings, before returning to Bath shed to have its fire dropped for the last time. Class 8F 48760 had the distinction of taking the final train of empty coal wagons up to the colliery on the 6.20am from Bath, returning later tender first with the last steam hauled coal train from Writhlington to Bath. As from the following Monday the coal would be taken out via Radstock over a newly laid spur onto the former Great Western Frome to Bristol line and be worked by diesel locomotives.

This day was also the end for Bath shed footplate crew Driver Norman Gibbons and Fireman Ryall, who were booked on the 6.45am Bath to Templecombe service and the return working at 2.00pm. Arriving at Templecombe at 8.29am they had a long layover in which to prepare for the return journey. As both crew members were rostered for "rest days" on the Saturday and Sunday, this northbound run would be their last turn on the footplate over the Mendips.

The final working on this Friday night was the 6.48pm through train from Bournemouth to Bath, which saw Salisbury based Battle of Britain Class 34057 "Biggin Hill" providing haulage throughout. This locomotive had run over the S&D before, but this working gave it the distinction of being the last Bullied Pacific used on a normal passenger service over the S&D. It was of course being worked up to Bath, in order to be ready for the final weekend of operations in which it would play a prominent part.

Taken from an up train at Radstock on 7th
February, with only four weeks of service left
passengers still seem quite numerous on what
looks to be a rather gloomy day.

Taken from Hinton Hill, an up local train hauled by 80043 approaches Hankley Wood in the week before final closure. At this point the train has not long left Wellow and is making its way below Twinhoe towards Midford, an exceptionally pretty stretch of the line.

John Spencer Gilks, courtesy ColourRail

**At Blandford on Saturday 19th February, Peter
was surprised at just how many passengers were
waiting as a down train ran in behind mogul
76011.**   Peter Barnfield.

Chapter Three

THE FINAL SATURDAY
5TH MARCH 1966

SATURDAY 5th MARCH 1966 was to be the last day of scheduled passenger services over the S&D, with two additional enthusiast specials, numerous light engine movements and a freight working out of Bath over the Midland Line to Bristol. Generally, all the trains ran well filled, with locals and enthusiasts who were saying farewell to a valued service or spending as much of the little remaining time available to ride over the S&D.

Early Morning Trains

At 6.39am on what was a cold and frosty morning a Hymek diesel arrived at Green Park with its passenger train, having made a thirty nine minute journey from Bristol Temple Meads. This service would give a connection into the 6.45am departure from Bath, the first of four timetabled passenger services to Templecombe on this final day of public services. The train was hauled by Standard 4MT mogul 76026 with Driver Doug Holden and Fireman Derek Coles on the footplate. Minus its smokebox numberplate and in a dirty run down condition, the Bournemouth based locomotive had a busy day ahead of it. Half an hour later the Hymek departed with the returning service to Bristol at 7.15am.

Meanwhile on the cold and misty Somerset Levels, Ivatt tank 41307 had set off from

Battle of Britain class "Biggin Hill" stands outside the S&D shed at Bath, prior to working light down to Evercreech Junction later in the morning to pick up the LCGB special.

Michael J. Chapman, www.railwayanamichael.com.

Highbridge for Templecombe with two coaches in tow on the 6.55am departure. The locomotive carried an S&D crest on a disc with blue background above its buffer beam to mark the end of the line.

At Bournemouth Central Standard 4MT Tank 80138 departed at 7.05am on the first service to Templecombe, whilst at Templecombe the start of the day's departures saw BR Standard 4MT Tank 80043 heading

48760 on the 8.15am service has just emerged from Combe Down tunnel and after passing the photographer will cross Tucking Mill viaduct on its way to Templecombe.

Don Froud.

48706 stands beneath the coaling stage at Bath prior to working the Great Western Society special that morning.

Michael J. Chapman, www.railwayanamichael.com.

The photographer stood back to record this more general scene of the S&D shed and the two locomotives, a number of other members of the public are also present.

Michael J. Chapman, www.railwayanamichael.com.

D828 "Magnificent" stands on the up line at Bath Green Park, with onlookers and the Midland engine shed visible in the background. It had brought the stock for the Great Western Society special over from Bristol.

Russell Leitch, courtesy ColourRail.

north on the 7.00am to Bath, and sister locomotive 80041 heading south at 7.35am, assisted down from Templecombe station to Number Two Junction by Ivatt Tank 41206. On the arrival of 41307 on the 6.55am from Highbridge at 8.05am, another of Templecombe's Ivatt tanks 41283 came off shed and went onto the rear of the two coaches from Highbridge, to form the return 8.20am service. Some ten minutes later 41206 provided assistance to 80138 and its train on the 7.05am from Bournemouth, drawing it back into Templecombe station where it arrived at 8.37am. Later that morning 41238 returned to Templecombe shed having run light from Highbridge after working the 8.20am service, passing through Evercreech Junction at 12.15pm.

Back at Bath driver Archie Gunning and fireman Alan Larcombe were in charge of 8F 48760 on the 8.15am service to Templecombe, formed of three Southern Region coaches. They had worked this turn all week except on Wednesday and Thursday which were their "rest days". Picking up the stock from one of the station's centre roads, the 8F ran out across the river bridge and then reversed the stock back into the station to form the train. On the platform were a good number of passengers who had been waiting from well before the departure time. The train arrived at Templecombe at 9.53am, and 48760 then ran light to Evercreech Junction where it was turned at 10.15am. The additional run was due to the fifty foot turntable at Templecombe being too small for the 8F,

whereas at fifty six feet the one at Evercreech would just accommodate it. This manoeuvre completed, the 8F waited until 10.45am when it worked to Templecombe shed yard to await its final duty on the 4.18pm departure to Bath.

At Bath 80043 had arrived on the 7.00am service from Templecombe and then retired to the shed to await its next working. Also on shed being prepared for their duties were Battle of Britain Class 34057 "Biggin Hill" and 8Fs 48309 and 48706, with Bath pilot locomotive Pannier tank 3681 also being in steam. Later in the morning "Biggin Hill" would run light to Evercreech Junction, to await the LCGB tour. Meanwhile 48309 would haul a loaded coal train to Bristol West Yard, before returning light engine to Bath later in the day. This was the same load of coal that 48706 had worked up to Bath from Writhlington Colliery on the previous day, being destined for Portishead power station. This was the last steam hauled freight train to leave Bath, and despite this went virtually unnoticed by the enthusiasts on the day. Steam heat fitted 48309 was used on this working despite having been requested for the Great Western Society special. Apparently the gear was defective and in the event the special was rostered to 48706. The day before volunteers from the Great Western Society cleaned the locomotive and painted white rings on its front buffers.

The Great Western Society Special
The stock for this eight coach special was hauled into Bath from Bristol Temple Meads by Plymouth Laira's Warship Class diesel locomotive D828 "Magnificent", the condition of the maroon coloured diesel fully living up to its name in the weak winter sunshine. The Society's headboard was placed on the 8F's lamp bracket below the chimney, meaning

76011 hauling the 9.37 from Bournemouth was running 3 minutes late, but still stopped long enough at Blandford for Nick Feast to get off the train and take a photograph. He was also very taken with the brand new Royal Enfield 250 Continental GT parked on the platform.   Nick Feast.

Fireman Chris Fell takes some air as 48706 climbs across Watery Bottom viaduct, hauling the Great Western Society special through Lyncombe Vale. The houses above the train are on Greenway Lane and the locomotive will continue to climb until just inside Combe Down tunnel, from where the line drops down to Midford.

Michael J. Chapman, www.railwayanamichael.com.

Having passed through Combe Down Tunnel and crossed Tucking Mill Viaduct, 48706 and its train passes the site of Midford goods yard, the smoke indicating that Chris Fell has just put some more coal on the fire for the climb ahead.

Don Froud

A short while afterwards, Don Foud captured "Biggin Hill" from the same position, running down light engine to Evercreech Junction.

Don Froud

35028 "Clan Line" is seen leaving Templecombe towards Bournemouth after earlier bringing the LCGB tour into the station.   Nick Feast

that the locomotive displayed the "normal" express headcode of two lamps on either side of the buffer beam. Crewed by driver Bill Gunning and Fireman Chris Fell, it departed from Green Park on schedule at 10.30am, running directly down to Bournemouth and not calling at Templecombe station.

I had booked to travel on this train, paying a fare of 25/0d for what would be my last S&D journey. Prior to joining the train at Green Park I went to Bath shed to observe what activity was taking place and photograph the remaining operational steam locomotives being prepared for their duties. As I mentioned in my introduction I lost my pictures years ago, but at a Bath Railway Society slide show given by Terry Nicholls I was surprised to see myself carefully composing a shot in one of his photographs!

48706 lumbered down to Bournemouth and I can recollect seeing many people standing on the lineside and at stations as we passed. Some took photographs, others waved, but some just stood watching solemnly as the train passed. On arrival at Bournemouth, the whole train seemed to disembark and head for the shed en masse - it was quite a sight. Our loco also went onto the shed to be turned and serviced before the run back to Bath and a return departure was made at 2.30pm. Progress was a little slow at times, particularly on the stretch up over the Mendips where the 1 in 50 gradient took its toll, and an enforced stop had to be made at Shepton Mallet for a "blow up" to raise more

48760 stands in the yard at Templecombe depot, awaiting its return to Bath on the 4.18pm service.   Nick Feast

steam. Chris Fell said that one reason for this was that on arriving at Bournemouth shed he declined taking on more coal for the journey back, but on returning to the loco he found the tender had been topped up with what proved to be inferior coal. Although Chris knew the S&D well from Bath to Templecombe, and had taken occasional workings as far as Blandford for fertilizer traffic, this was to be both his first and last turn to Bournemouth and back.

The LCGB Special

The second special train on this final Saturday was "The Somerset & Dorset Rail Tour" organised by the Locomotive Club of Great Britain. 35028 "Clan Line" departed from Waterloo on time at 8.55am, and ran directly down the Southern main line. It arrived on time at Templecombe, where two Ivatt Tanks 41249 and 41307 were waiting to take the train forwards. Departing at 11.19pm it ran to Evercreech Junction and then across the Levels to Highbridge, making a ten minute photographic stop at Glastonbury along the route. The train next returned to Evercreech Junction, where two immaculate Bulleid Pacifics were waiting in the centre road to take over for the run over the Mendips to Bath. 34006 "Bude" with white painted buffers had worked light engine from Bournemouth shed, running through Broadstone at 12.25pm, near which point it passed "Clan Line" running back to Bournemouth. "Biggin Hill" had worked light engine from Bath and was photographed running tender first past Midford goods yard by Don Froud.

The LCGB tour departed from Evercreech Junction five minutes ahead of its booked time at 2.05pm, so that an additional photographic stop could be made at Chilcompton. 34006 "Bude", crewed by driver Donald

Pannier tank 3681 draws the stock of the RCTS special out of Green Park station to release the two Bulleid Pacifics for servicing.

Beale and fireman Tom Upshall, was coupled ahead of 34057 "Biggin Hill" with driver Albert Williams at its regulator. The special ran in to Bath Green Park at 3.11pm, where Pannier 3681 shunted the stock out of the station, releasing the pacifics for turning and servicing on Bath shed. It is understood that this was the only work that 3681 did as the Bath pilot locomotive on this day.

At 4.07pm, seventeen minutes behind schedule, "Bude" and "Biggin Hill" departed from Green Park for the return over the Mendips. It was further delayed by an unscheduled photographic stop at Shepton Mallet and then another stop was made at Evercreech Junction for both locos to take

on water. Arriving at Bournemouth at 6.51pm, "Clan Line" then took over for the run back to Waterloo. Suffering a further sixty minutes of delays the train eventually arrived in the Capital at 10.10pm, ninety minutes behind schedule.

Evercreech and the Branch

Earlier on at Evercreech, the two Ivatt tanks that had brought the LCGB tour back to the Junction had been split from from each other. 41249 ran back along the branch to work the 4.00pm service from Highbridge while 41307 waited for the 2.00pm departure from Templecombe to arrive. At 2.23pm the Bath train arrived headed by Standard 4MT 80138,

34057 "Biggin Hill" has its sandboxes filled at
Bath shed after bringing the LCGB special to
Bath with 34006 "Bude".   Stewart Blencowe.

and 41307 moved out on to the main line and ran forwards on to the front of 80138, which it then led bunker first back to Bath. This was done to work the Ivatt tank off the line and resulted in a slightly delayed departure, but the train still arrived back at Bath in the daylight, where 41307 was immediately withdrawn from service.

Driver Clarence Rawles and fireman Tony Rossiter were the crew on the 4.00pm off Highbridge, the departure of which was delayed as a Hymek diesel had been used on the milk train at Bason Bridge and had taken longer than usual to run round its train. On this last occasion the service was extended beyond Evercreech to Templecombe, a decision made locally by the crews and signalmen and not by the Western Region control.

Bath Afternoon
While the LCGB special had been traversing the branch, at Green Park Hymek D7000 had arrived on the Saturdays only 12.10pm service from Bristol Temple Meads. After a quick run round its three coach stock, D7000 then took the well filled 1.00pm service back to Bristol Temple Meads. These two workings formed the final timetabled passenger services to operate in each direction along the former Midland route. During the run back to Bristol the Hymek and its train was passed near Kelston by 8F 48309, running tender first to Bath shed and withdrawal, after earlier hauling its coal train to Bristol. On reaching Fishponds station the train set off the many detonators that had been placed along the track, and D7000 repeatedly sounded its horn to further mark the passing of the last service.

A further Hymek diesel was to be seen several hours later on the Midland line, when D7030 worked empty coaching stock into Bath Green Park from Weston-super-Mare in readiness for the SLS special over the S&D on

48309 runs light through Mangotsfield on its way back to Bath after earlier working its coal train to Bristol West depot.   Stewart Blencowe.

the following day. After depositing the stock in one of the centre roads, the diesel then took the return coaches from the Great Western Society's special back to Bristol. This was the train upon which I had earlier travelled from Bournemouth, arriving back at Green Park just after 6.00pm.

Templecombe Movements
Standard 4 mogul 76011 worked the 09.37am Bournemouth to Templecombe where it was assisted into the station by Ivatt tank 41307, for a scheduled arrival at 11.03am. It then returned to Bournemouth on the 12.30pm departure and after a wait was used on the 3.43pm (Saturdays only) to Blandford. After arrival and running round, 76011 worked the

stock empty to Bailey Gate station from where it formed the 6.32pm service to Bournemouth. Seen off by a large crowd of locals, this was the penultimate Down service to call at the station. As previously mentioned, unkempt Standard 4MT mogul 76026 had worked the 6.45am service from Bath to Templecombe. From here it worked the 9.05am service to Branksome, with Driver Trevor Netley and Fireman Mike Baker on the footplate, being assisted from the station to Number Two Junction by Ivatt tank 41206. It was next used on the 1.25pm Branksome to Templecombe service, carrying members of the Oxford University Railway Society who had added their own specially made headboard to the locomotive. After arrival at

The 2.00pm departure from Templecombe approaches Radstock station, headed by Standard 4MT 80138 with Ivatt tank 41307 coupled in front of it.

Michael J. Chapman, www.railwayanamichael.com.

Templecombe at 2.42pm 76026 continued on the 3.30pm service to Evercreech Junction. Here it was turned in readiness to work the 4.13pm back to Templecombe, subsequently forming the 4.42pm departure for Bournemouth. 76026 was the final locomotive to be turned at Evercreech Junction and the return run to Bournemouth was to be its last over the S&D before closure.

At Templecombe, the Oxford University Railway Society and their headboard transferred to the 4.18pm Bath service, hauled by 48760 with three Mk 1 coaches. This train had two signal checks at Evercreech Junction and was held up again south of Binegar, where it was passed by 34006 "Bude" and 34057 "Biggin Hill" on the southbound LCGB special, with much whistling taking place between the locos. At Binegar station it passed 80043 standing at the down platform with the 4.25pm service from Bath. After arrival at Green Park, 48760 made its way to the shed where it was turned and backed down on to a siding. It was kept in light steam overnight as it was acting as standby locomotive for the following day's special working.

Final Daytime Departure

After working the first train of the day, departing from Templecombe at 7.00am, 4MT tank 80043 spent the day resting on Bath shed until later in the afternoon, when it backed down to the station to take the 4.25pm service to Templecombe. Driver Cecil Waldron and fireman Wayne Mayo were on the footplate, and had worked this service through the preceding week, except for Thursday which had been their rest day. The guard in charge of the train was John Hopkin. The locomotive carried an improvised headboard made by a Paul Payne, together with an S&D crest mounted on a Southern headcode disc. The locomotive crew were not alone on

Ivatt tank 41206 approaches Midford viaduct from the south. It followed the 2.00pm departure from Templecombe up the line to Bath and withdrawal. Don Froud.

the footplate for this run, as enthusiasts were being given the opportunity to ride in the cab. This was the last down run from Bath to be made in daylight and the three coach train was accordingly packed to capacity. A report from one of the enthusiasts on the footplate said they had to cling on for dear life as the train headed for Evercreech at speeds in excess of 60mph! However they all made it safely to Templecombe, where the train arrived well in advance of the 5.37pm service from Bournemouth. This service was hauled by classmate 80037, again with a three coach set well filled with passengers. After being detached from its train, 80037 remained at Templecombe to pilot the last southbound departure to Number Two Junction, before

making its final journey back to Bath light engine where it was withdrawn from service. Other Templecombe allocated locomotives which made similar journeys on this day included 41206 and 41296. 41206 was observed passing through Midford at around 3.45pm, while 41296 was seen heading north through Binegar at about 7.00pm.

Last Branch Train

Back at Evercreech Junction, the final service over the branch to Highbridge was due to depart at 5.15pm but starting from Templecombe rather than Evercreech, it set off somewhat later. This was due to the 4.00pm from Highbridge continuing through to Templecombe, as noted earlier. Ivatt tank

"Biggin Hill" reverses towards Green Park station to couple up to the LCGB special, being watched by Gordon King of the British Transport police, on hand to hold back the crowds.   Nick Feast.

At 4.19pm "Bude" and "Biggin Hill" cross Midford Viaduct at the head of the southbound LCGB special.

Don Froud

The shadows are lengthening on Ivatt tank 41429 as it prepares to stop at Bason Bridge with the 4.00pm departure from Highbridge.

Rev. John Sutters, courtesy Phil Sutters.

48760 on the 4.15pm departure from Templecombe heads north near Wincanton, it carries a headboard for the Oxford University Railway Society whose members were on board.

Trevor Owen, courtesy ColourRail.

80043 heads the 4.15pm service over Midford viaduct. People are crowded inside the train, which was the last daytime departure from Bath on this day.

Don Froud.

Hymek D7030 makes ready to depart from Green Park with the empty stock from the Great Western Society special. On the right can be seen the stock for the Sunday SLS train.

Michael J. Chapman. www.railwayanamichael.com.

Pat Dorland, one time bandsman and publican of the "Royal Arms", plays the "Last Post" as the final service train for Bath departs Templecombe.

Rodney Scovell, courtesy Ian Matthews.

41249 ran to Highbridge bunker first, with a wreath on the top centre bracket of the bunker. This had been made by schoolgirl Linda Stowe, daughter of the Evercreech Junction Station Master Alex Stowe. On its buffer beam the locomotive also sported an S&D crest on a Southern headcode disc. The loco took water at Evercreech before setting off with its two crowded coaches for Glastonbury, where a large crowd and the local press were waiting to record the event. As the train departed into the gathering darkness, cheers from those on the platform competed with the locomotive's whistle and explosions from detonators placed on the track. On arrival at Highbridge, and after the train had been emptied of its passengers, the

two coaches were taken across the Western Region main line and placed in a siding in the Up Western yard. In darkness and without ceremony, 41249 then made its way back across the Levels to the shed at Templecombe for one final night.

Final Workings

The last timetabled passenger trains to run over the S&D were the 6.10pm from Bath to Templecombe and the 6.46pm from Bournemouth to Bath. On this Saturday both these trains were also used to clear coaching stock from earlier workings. The 6.10pm service had 80138 at its head, with Templecombe's driver George Welch, fireman Bruce Briant and guard Reg Brewer working

their final turn back to their home station. In the opposite direction 80041 headed the 6.46pm from Bournemouth to Bath, driver Les Cuss, fireman Tony Axford and guard Edward Schovell all working back to Templecombe on this service. On arrival 80043 was used as pilot locomotive to haul the train up from Number Two Junction to the station, where the coaches from the earlier 4.25pm from Bath were added to the train. When the 6.10pm service from Bath arrived at Templecombe, the coaches from the earlier 5.37pm from Bournemouth were also added to work them off the S&D to Bournemouth.

With the final northbound train now consisting of six coaches, 80041 was placed in front of 80043 and 15 year old Christopher Caines and 16 year old John Miller from Millborne Port placed laurel wreaths on the leading locomotive's smokebox. Due to this and extra shunting operations, the train departed Templecombe some 25 minutes late at 8.45pm. It left to the accompaniment of exploding detonators placed along the track and the "Last Post" played on a bugle by Pat Dorland, one time RAF bandsman and landlord of the "Royal Hotel". On arrival at Evercreech Junction, a coffin was placed in the guards compartment and a further wreath fixed to the smokebox of 80041. The Evercreech Junction staff, Station Master Alec Stowe, Charlie Vaughan, Eddie Riggs and Vic Freak all turned out smartly dressed to the last, and there were certainly tears in some of their eyes. Despite the lateness and the dark, many people along the line turned out to witness the passing of this train. Peter James used this service to return to his school at Downside after a day witnessing the last rites, and in alighting at Chilcompton became the last person to use the station. At Radstock numerous detonators had been placed on the

line and as the train left for Bath the resulting explosions echoed off the surrounding hills, disturbing the quiet of the winter evening in the small town. Approaching Bath the peace was shattered on exiting Devonshire tunnel, as both locomotives had their whistles held wide open on the run down through the suburbs of Oldfield Park, past Bath Junction signal box and into Bath Green Park station. The train arrived at 10.52pm, just over an hour later than scheduled and, although I was not there to witness it, I can well remember the haunting sounds of the whistles being amplified across the bowl of the City as this final passenger service arrived. The journey was also the last to be made by 80041 in steam, and its fire was dropped for the final time on return to Bath shed and withdrawal from service.

The six coaches of the corresponding last Down train from Templecombe to Bournemouth departed at 9.03pm, hauled by 80138 with Albert Kiddle and fireman J. Parkes on the footplate, all working their way back to their home shed. The train was drawn back to Number Two Junction by 80037 which then made its way to Bath, making it

the final northbound movement of the day and the last train to pass Evercreech North signal box before it mysteriously burnt down that night. By now only two operational locomotives remained at Templecombe shed, Ivatt tanks 41249 and 41283, which would be used on the following day's special over the branch. Withdrawn BR Standard 4MTs 75072 and 75073 were the only other locomotives present at Templecombe, placed in a siding awaiting onward movement to a scrapyard at Ringwood.

80138 carried a wreath on its smokebox door and at Templecombe a destination board proclaiming "Waterloo" was added to the top of the smokebox. Along the route the local communities again came out in force to watch the train make its last stops, particularly at Sturminster Newton, Blandford Forum and Broadstone, the local press also recording its passing. I have been told that on the journey from Templecombe to Bournemouth this train failed to carry a red tail lamp, as it had been taken by a souvenir hunter – if this was the case, I wonder whether the signalmen along the route queried it?

Chapter Four

THE FINAL SUNDAY
6TH MARCH 1966

FOR THE FINAL operational day of the S&D a special working timetable was issued by the Divisional Managers Office at Bristol. This was dated 3rd March, marked 'Private and Not for Publication' and stamped 'Bath Station Mid Rly'. It covered two enthusiast specials together with associated light engine movements, connecting trains and the Bason Bridge milk train.

The two railtours were operated by the RCTS and the SLS, starting at London Waterloo and Bath Green Park respectively, with a connecting DMU running from Birmingham to Bath and return.

SLS Departure
At Bath shed that morning a large number of newly withdrawn locomotives were lined up in the various sidings alongside piles of ash, some of the locomotives still warm from the previous day's activities. On the shed 8F 48706 and Standard 4MT 80043 were being prepared to work their final duty under the watchful eye of acting shed foreman Dave Massey. Both locomotives had received some attention by the shed cleaners as they were to be used on the SLS special, 80043 being coupled inside 48706 to provide steam heating. The ten coaches for this train had been worked into Bath on the previous afternoon by D7030, and it was clearly stated in

the working timetable that "Special Attention had to be given to the Cleaning, Watering and Steam Heating of this Train". An interesting instruction given that the previous day's Great Western Society tour had run without any heating. As the two engines backed down to Green Park station, crowds of enthusiasts lined the tracks, standing on all available vantage

Photo: I. Peters.   *Block Courtesy: Railway Magazine.*
53807, the (then) sole survivor of the S.D.J.R. class 7F 2-8-0s at Masbury summit with the 8.55 a.m. down freight from Bath on the last day of its service, 5th September, 1962.

Photographic Souvenir
in connection with

LAST PASSENGER TRAIN
on the
Bath — Templecombe — Bournemouth Section
SUNDAY, 6th MARCH, 1966
Organised by the STEPHENSON LOCOMOTIVE SOCIETY
(Midland Area)

points in order to witness and record the happenings on this very last day.

At 7.58am a six car formation of two Metropolitan Cammell DMUs (M50325, M59118 and M50307, together with M50329, M59122 and M50311) left Birmingham New Street station bound for Bath, picking up passengers at Cheltenham Spa and Gloucester Eastgate and arriving at Green Park at 10.15am.

On time at 10.30am, 48706 and 80043 (train reporting code 1X06) eased out of Green Park station for the southbound run to Bournemouth. 48706 carried an "SLS Special" headboard on its buffer beam, so the unique S&D passenger train headlamp code could be displayed. This day was to be a final double act for the Gunning brothers with Archie driving 48706 and his brother Bill driving 80043, supported by firemen Dave Norman and Albert Parsons respectively. The locomotive cabs were rather crowded as several enthusiasts had managed to get footplate rides. These including a good friend of mine the late John James, who can be seen squeezed inside the cab of 80043 in a photograph taken just after departure from Bath. Time was lost between Midford and Midsomer Norton, as the train had to set back on to the Up line at Writhlington and run "wrong road" to Midsomer Norton. This was

It is nearly 10.30am on Sunday and the SLS special is ready to depart from Green Park. At its head is 8F 48706 with Standard 4 tank 80043 coupled inside to provide steam heating to the train.

due to engineering works south of Radstock, where the Down line of the S&D was being slewed on to a new connection to the parallel GWR Frome to Bristol route. This would enable coal trains from Writhlington Colliery to continue operating from the next day via this route instead of the S&D. Shepton Mallet was reached sixteen minutes late where a photographic stop was made. A further delay was encountered as the train approached Evercreech Junction as the signal box there had mysteriously burnt down in the middle of the night, requiring trains to be hand signalled through the junction with flags. Water was taken by both locomotives at Evercreech Junction station, the train departing at 12.18pm and by now running 22 minutes behind schedule. Some fast running from here saw the train arriving at Templecombe at 12.25pm for a shorter than booked stop. Ivatt tank 41249 was attached at the rear to haul the train back down to Number Two Junction. This was the last occasion on which this time consuming manoeuvre was made, and it was widely reported that 41249 was manned by the Templecombe shedmaster Harry Jeans, working alone. After 41249 was detached, the train set off southwards again, the Ivatt returning to the shed to await its duty on the RCTS special. Blandford was reached on schedule at 1.06pm but there was then a delay until shortly after the late running RCTS special had arrived at 1.29pm, allowing just enough time for passengers to disembark and photograph the historic scene. Setting off at 1.32pm, some fifteen minutes later the train passed 34057 "Biggin Hill" on its way up to Bath, from where it would later work the RCTS special south together with "Okehampton". Bournemouth Central was reached twenty seven minutes late at 2.09pm, with the majority of the passengers heading for the nearby shed where nearly forty loco-

motives were observed. The stock from the special was taken to Bournemouth East sidings, 48706 going to the shed for servicing while 80043 hauled the stock back into Bournemouth Central, before it also went for servicing.

The RCTS Special

Billed as the "Somerset & Dorset Farewell Rail Tour", this train departed from Waterloo station at 9.00am behind Merchant Navy 35028 "Clan Line", running west via Twickenham and then the Mid Hants route owing to Sunday engineering work. At Bournemouth Central the crews were changed, with Bournemouth based driver Johnny Walker and fireman Tony White taking over for the run up the S&D. Leaving Bournemouth one minute late at 12.17pm, the train apparently had to stop at Branksome to replace a steam pipe, resulting in a delayed arrival at Broadstone. Here a longer than scheduled photographic stop saw a departure

at 1.05pm, nearly half an hour behind schedule. After the stop at Blandford, the train got away at 1.35pm and managed to regain some time before arriving at Templecombe Number Two Junction at 2.00pm, twenty two minutes behind schedule.

After being replaced on the train by the Ivatt tanks "Clan Line" retired to the shed for servicing. When the final hoist of coal was dropped into the tender by shedman Ernie Caulley, the Merchant Navy became the last engine to use Templecombe shed for locomotive purposes.

Meanwhile Ivatt tank 41283, sporting white painted buffers and with driver Fritz Lawrence and fireman Dennis Nettley on the footplate, had been coupled up to classmate 41249 ready for the run to Highbridge. Following a smart change of locomotives, the special got underway at 2.08pm. An eight minute stop was made at Evercreech Junction before the Special became the final passenger carrying train to traverse the branch to

The signal has cleared and the locomotives are getting the train on the move. Each had crowded footplates, the author's friend John James travelled on 80043 and appears to be clearing something from his eye.

The special looks to be making good progress as it emerges from Combe Down tunnel, in the background can be seen the derelict De Montalt Mill.

Don Froud.

Highbridge, arriving at the S&D station at 3.19pm. Here all the passengers had to leave the train, taking the opportunity to photograph the shunting movements before making their way to the Down main line platform. The two tank locomotives drew the stock across the main line and into the Great Western goods shed road, before setting back into the Down platform, ready for departure towards Bristol headed by 34013 "Okehampton".

This locomotive was provided by Salisbury shed and according to the working timetable had left there at 11.30am, running light engine to Bristol East Depot via Westbury and Bath Spa. Following a crew change, 34013 was turned using the Rhubarb Loop at North Somerset Junction and then ran tender first to Highbridge. Water was taken at Temple Meads from 1.49pm to 1.57pm. I've not found any record of these movements until the locomotive arrived at Temple Meads station, but as one friend observed you could have sent "Lode Star" or a Dean Goods through Bath Spa that day and nobody would have noticed, as everyone was at Green Park photographing the S&D. "Okehampton" ran into the down goods loop at Highbridge at 3.00pm, to wait there for the arrival of the Special at 3.19pm.

At 3.41pm, just six minutes behind schedule, "Okehampton" and its train eased out of the down platform at Highbridge station, crossed over to the up line and headed north back to Temple Meads. The train passed through Bristol Temple Meads without stopping, and then the West Country Class "dug in" for the climb up through Staple Hill to Mangotsfield station. Here it swung north at the junction towards Gloucester, before stopping on the Midland main line well clear of Mangotsfield North Junction. Bristol Bath Road based Hymek D7014 came on to the rear of the train from the Bath direction, while

"Clan Line" is pictured at Broadstone, where it halted for fifteen minutes for photographs before departing north at 1.05pm.

34013 was uncoupled. The Hymek took the special onwards, running south to the East Junction and on to Green Park, where it arrived at 4.54pm. "Okehampton" followed to Bath, taking on water on arrival before backing down onto 34057 "Biggin Hill" and its train, standing in the departure platform.

At 5.24pm 34013 "Okehampton" and 34057 "Biggin Hill" pulled out of Bath Green Park station with the last southbound passenger train to traverse the line to Templecombe. Within two minutes the train had swung onto the S&D at Bath Junction, with the crews of both locos determined to make this a memorable run. One eye witness who was at Bath Junction remembered "Okehampton" spitting fire into the sky.

Further up Devonshire bank both locomotives were throwing large volumes of smoke into the evening sky as the crews built up their fires. Midford station was reached within ten minutes of departure from Bath, but there followed an unscheduled ten minute stop to allow photography in the failing light. Photographers swarmed across the track and clambered on every possible vantage point, including the signals. The stop was made on the pretext of signalman Percy Savage cautioning the crews on the "wrong line" working from Writhlington to Midsomer Norton. With their fires built up for a last assault over the Mendips, both locomotives were blowing off furiously before the signals were finally cleared.

The two specials met at Blandford station where they stopped for photographs to be taken. The SLS train is about to depart in this view taken at about 1.30pm.　　　　　　　RCTS

Once beyond Midsomer Norton, those who witnessed the special head up over the Mendips described the performance as "volcanic", with fire and cinders being thrown high into the night sky. One railway publication described the sight as an "unforgettable firework display". The crew on "Biggin Hill" were driver Peter Guy and fireman Mike Standhaft from Bournemouth shed, accompanied by a Western Region Traction Inspector. The crew of 34013 "Okehampton" were driver Arthur Hatcher and a young fireman, both from Templecombe shed. Mike Standhaft commented to me that the Western Inspector turned a blind eye as both crews "went for it". The inspector crossed over to Mike and said that he'd seen engines being "lifted" in his

time, but never anything like that night's performance. This last southbound train passed over Masbury Summit at an unheard of 51mph. Giving an S&D slide show to a railway society years later, an audience member who had been a passenger on the train confirmed in no uncertain terms that it had indeed been a very lively and memorable display from the two Bulleid pacifics.

"Okehampton" and "Biggin Hill" arrived at Templecombe at 7.04pm, running right through the station and coming to a halt out towards the far end of the yard to the west of the station, where they were uncoupled from the train. Meanwhile "Clan Line" made its way up from the shed and ran through the S&D platform as far as the other end of the train, where it was coupled up ready for

departure. At 7.17pm, just nine minutes behind its booked time, "Clan Line" crossed over from the yard to the main line and departed eastwards for Waterloo, finally arriving there at 9.36pm. After a crew change, "Okehampton" also departed eastwards to its home depot at Salisbury and the relieved crew made their way back to the shed where they became the very last locomen to sign off at Templecombe motive power depot.

SLS Return

The last northbound passenger train to run over the S&D departed from Bournemouth Central at 4.20pm, an hour later than its booked time. It was worked back by the same Bath crews as on the outward run and the guard was Bernard Ware. At Blandford a stop was made for 80043 to take on water, but at Templecombe the special ran straight through without stopping. The next stop was at Evercreech Junction where both locomotives took on water, leaving the train straddling the level crossing for twelve minutes. The southbound RCTS special headed by the hard working 34013 "Okehampton" and 34057 "Biggin Hill" was passed at Moorewood, with all the locomotives' whistles sounding. On the approach to Radstock, Hymek D7018 was passed on the newly ballasted chord line to the Great Western route. Les Willsher signalled the train through Radstock as he worked the very last shift in Radstock North Box. The gates would be disconnected and operated by hand for the freight workings from the following day.

This final special drew in to the south platform at Bath Green Park station at 6.51pm. With 80043 coupled inside, 48706 stood at the buffer stops with a wreath on its smokebox door and proudly displaying the S&D headcode. Those tour participants who were travelling back to Birmingham made

The yard at Templecombe pictured some time after 2.00pm, the two Standard 4 locomotives would be moved to Blandford that night and the wisps of steam visible are from "Clan Line" being serviced inside the shed.

The LCGB train has arrived at Highbridge and passengers watch as preparations are made to shunt the stock over to the Great Western side of the station. Rev. John Sutters, courtesy Phil Sutters.

The stock of the RCTS train is drawn in to the Great Western goods yard, from where it will set back into the down platform on the main line.

their way over to the station's north platform, where the six car DMU was waiting. Due to depart at 6.26pm, it was swiftly despatched, forming the last passenger carrying train to work out of Bath Green Park over the Midland line to Mangotsfield. As the train left it passed Hymek D7014, waiting to remove the carriages from the special and take it empty stock to Bristol St. Philip's Marsh, where Bath guard Bernard Ware would hand over to Harry Palmer. Once the stock had departed, 48706 and 80043 made their way

coupled together back to the shed, with the crews being joined by a large number of enthusiasts on each footplate. The locos were split and, despite the fact there was no further use for them, turned in time honoured fashion on Bath's turntable before their fires were dropped and the two crews signed off for a final time.

Supporting Movements
By the time that 48706 and 80043 arrived back at Bath, Ivatt tanks 41249 and 41283

were already on shed, their work also done. They had run back to Bath from Highbridge via Temple Meads.

After positioning the stock of the RCTS special at Highbridge, the two Ivatt tanks shunted back onto S&D tracks for one final revenue earning turn. This was the Bason Bridge to Highbridge milk train, which on this occasion ran an hour later than shown in the working timetable. The Western Region authorities had not wanted this steam working to take place and requested a diesel

The shunt involved taking the train through the
goods shed, in the background 34013 is waiting
in the down loop to take the special back to Bath
via Bristol.

**"Okehampton" gets the RCTS away from
Highbridge.**   J.J. Smith, courtesy Bluebell Archive.

"Okehampton" and "Biggin Hill" wait for departure in the failing light at Midford. On the left can be seen the photographer's son John, who comments: "*I have little recollection of the junior form of myself, winding on my Kodak Brownie and getting into position to take a final photograph of Okehampton and Biggin Hill at 5.30pm on that Sunday*". Don Froud.

be used. Despite this, it had been scheduled in the special working timetable as a steam working, using one locomotive from the pair that had hauled the RCTS special. In the event it was decided by those on the ground to use both locomotives which, with two brake vans in tow, ran to Bason Bridge to collect the loaded milk tanks. Not only was it very rare for this working to be double headed, but this was to be the last steam hauled freight to be operated by the Western Region. On arrival at Highbridge, and without ceremony, the milk tanks were left in the yard for later collection and 41249 and 41283 made their way to Bath. It is not known who crewed the locos for this journey, but it would have been a very long turn of duty for the Templecombe men, who also wouldn't have known the route. Whoever they were, on arrival at Bath a number of individuals climbed down from the locomotives and immediately made their way over to Bath Spa station to catch trains.

The Final Act

34057 "Biggin Hill" ran back down to the S&D and coupled up to the two Standard locomotives standing in the shed yard, ready to haul them to Blandford on the first part of their journey to Ringwood for scrapping. Both locomotives had been oiled up at Templecombe shed by fitter's mate Frank Ray as a precaution against running hot during their journey. Fireman Mike Standhaft recalls that it felt strange running down towards the empty shed, with the lights still burning and a solitary shedman remaining on duty. "Biggin Hill" hauled the two Standards out of the yard and on to the main line before running round and setting off towards Bournemouth at 7.06pm. These were the last signalled movements at Templecombe before the signalman signed off from duty and Number Two

Junction signal box closed forever. With no brake van in the formation, driver Johnny Walker and fireman Tony White each took to the footplate of one of the Standards to act as brakeman. This was also a way of returning them to their home shed of Bournemouth. One odd aspect is that the movement of the two Standards had not been detailed in the special operating instructions for the day, which showed 34057 "Biggin Hill" running back light engine to Bournemouth.

At Sturminster Newton station the convoy was met by the local press from the Western Gazette who interviewed the crews, but other than this the working passed almost unnoticed.

On arrival at Blandford 75072 and 75073 were left near bridge 197, just to the south of the station. "Biggin Hill" then continued light engine with a very full cab. Driver Peter Guy and fireman Mike Standaft were joined by Johnny Walker and Tony White plus a sixteen year old John Antell, who was dropped off at Bailey Gate station. John later became well known in railway preservation as a haulier who, for forty years until retirement in 2014, transported railway locomotives around the country by road. The passing of "Biggin Hill" from the S&D at Broadstone was recorded in the signal box register at 10.40pm, considerably later than its booked time. The box consequently had to stay open

The gas lamps at Bath Green Park are lit as the Metropolitan Cammell DMU waits for its passengers from the late running SLS special.

Trevor Owen, courtesy ColourRail.

much later than planned for its passage.

"Biggin Hill" thus became the last locomotive to run on the Somerset & Dorset system before closure officially took place at midnight on Sunday 6th of March.

Biggin Hill

This locomotive earned a special place in my personal railway history by providing me with my last steam haulage under British Railways. In February 1967 I went to Bath Spa station to catch the 1.12pm Portsmouth Harbour to Cardiff service, only to discover it was running late due to a locomotive failure. As the train ran in, I saw to my great delight and surprise that instead of the usual Hymek, the train was hauled by 34057 "Biggin Hill". I expect the locomotive had been put on the train at Salisbury, but whatever the reason and despite it being only a short trip, it put in a good turn of speed on the run over to Bristol. I didn't realise at the time that this would be my last steam run under BR, but I still have a very clear vision of that day. After arrival at Temple Meads it was swiftly despatched light engine back to the Southern.

The loco went on to haul several railtours in early 1967, before being withdrawn at Salisbury shed at the beginning of May, the last original Battle of Britain Class to be taken out of service. It was subsequently moved to Nine Elms shed for storage as a possible candidate for preservation. However this was not to be and in October it was towed away to South Wales and cut up at Cashmores of Newport.

"Biggin Hill" pictured inside Nine Elms shed on 6th July 1967. The locomotive has had one of its cylinders and motion taken apart, possibly for donation to "Blackmore Vale", out of sight on the next track.   Brian Dale.

Chapter Five

AFTER CLOSURE

ON THE MORNING of Monday 7th of March 1966 stations were deserted and signal boxes stood unattended, their clocks still telling the right time and train registers left open on desks. None of this would matter anymore, the line was dead.

The last rites of the line were well documented in the press. The "Bath Evening Chronicle", "Western Daily Press" and "Western Gazette" all carried stories and photographs of the last trains and readers bemoaned the closure in the letters pages. Photographic spreads in the railway press followed, "The Railway Magazine" and "Railway World" covering the line and its closure in some detail. The RCTS magazine "The Railway Observer" came out in the following May, and gave a detailed account of the last operations and the special train the Society had run on the final day. Both the BBC and ITV had sent film crews out to record the last trains, and I can still remember seeing film of the station staff at Evercreech Junction carrying a coffin on to the last up scheduled passenger train on the BBC news on Monday evening.

Some sections of the S&D remained open for freight traffic, with the longest being that from Broadstone to Blandford. This was kept operational for general goods together with fertiliser and military traffic for the nearby Blandford Camp. A short part of the branch from Highbridge still saw milk traffic from the dairy at Bason Bridge, while coal from Writhlington Colliery to Portishead Power Station was worked back along the S&D to Radstock, continuing to Bristol via the newly laid spur line. A short section in the City of Bath was also retained for coal traffic, skirting the suburb of Oldfield Park as far as the Co-op dairy siding at Melcombe Road. Bath Yard remained quite busy, seeing regular coal deliveries for Bath Gasworks and considerable traffic for engineering firm Stothert and Pitt. Paper was still handled in the goods shed for a nearby printing press, various timber yards still used rail for deliveries and some general freight traffic remained. Stotherts even did their own shunting within their extensive works, using a steam crane which is now preserved at the entrance to the Western Riverside development.

Ivatt tank 41283 was briefly put into steam at Green Park in the days after closure and is seen here hauling 48760 out of the yard during March 1966.

**Hymek D7043 hauls withdrawn steam
locomotives away from Green Park shed on 18th
March 1966.**   Stewart Blencowe.

Ex Bath Pannier on display at the Bath Road
open day on 30th April, partial cleaning has
revealed a smart British Railways crest from
beneath the grime.   Frank Toon.

Locomotives withdrawn from Bath shed are seen stored at St Phillips Marsh, in the background is the site of the Midland station and goods yard.

Stewart Blencowe.

48706 on display at a Bath Road open day on 30th April 1966, complete with the headboard it had carried on the 5th March.

Remaining Staff

The closure meant great upheaval for the local railwaymen, many of whom had worked on the line for all their working lives. During the last week of operation there were twenty five drivers and twenty seven firemen still employed at Bath shed. Some were made redundant, others retired and a number continued their railway careers elsewhere. For example Chris Fell, fireman on the Great Western Society special on the Saturday, reported to Southall shed from the following Monday. However, some members of the original staff were retained, reporting for duty at Bath Green Park on the 7th.

From the 7th March, Bath Green Park and the Midland Goods Yard came under the administration of the Area Manager at Bath Spa. A few shunters and signalmen remained on the payroll at Green Park, as were some staff in the footplate grades. The latter were retained until the end of April to clear the site and prepare withdrawn locomotives for onward movement. I visited the shed on the Tuesday afternoon following closure and it was certainly a hive of activity.

Staff also remained at Blandford under the jurisdiction of the Southern Region, the signal box and goods office both staying open in the short term. The box at Broadstone also remained operational to control the junction of the S&D to Blandford and the freight only line to Wimborne and Ringwood, which had lost its passenger service back in 1964.

Ex Templecombe 4MTs 75072 and 75073 stand at Ringwood station yard in April 1966, where they were cut up by scrap merchants Thomas Ward & Co. Nick Feast

At Radstock, the box closed and the S&D level crossing gates were now manually operated by the train crew. Radstock shed continued in use to stable a shunter and both drivers and yard staff remained, now coming under Western Region management at Bristol. On the S&D side there was coal from Writhlington and rolling stock and materials to and from the British Wagon Works. Meanwhile, the Western yard handled traffic from Kilmersdon Colliery and the extensive Marcroft wagon repair workshops. Permanent way gangs were retained at Radstock and Templecombe, continuing to maintain the S&D track for the first six months after closure. A further gang at Broadstone maintained the line from Blandford Forum to Holes Bay Junction.

Bath Steam

As I had witnessed on the Tuesday following closure, plenty of work remained to be done. The rows of withdrawn and redundant locomotives needed to be oiled, have their connecting rods removed and be shunted into position ready to be hauled away for scrapping. Number plates and works plates were also removed and piled up in the shed outside the foreman's office. When I visited the shed on that Tuesday I was able to purchase the number plate from Bath's 8F 48760 for the sum of £2. I treasure it to this day, along with an 82F Green Park shed code plate which I bought a few years later - paying much more than I had for the number plate! The Bath Railway Society acquired the chair used by the former Bath Green Park shedmaster Harold Morris and this is brought out from time to time on special occasions by the Society.

Over the years a story has circulated that on Monday 7th a locomotive was put into steam and sent down the S&D to collect

On the afternoon of 26th February 1967, the crew watch their locomotive carefully as it negotiates the trackwork at Bailey Gate. D6551 is in the process of running round the six wheeled van it had brought up from the Poole direction.
Tim Chapman.

redundant station fittings. A subsequent statement from relief Area Manager Ian Vaughan confirmed the run, the locomotive used apparently being a Pannier tank. I've not been able to add any more information to this, but the late Russell Leitch photographed 3681 in steam on the 7th, which at least supports the story. Another reason for the steaming was to check the locomotive over, as along with classmate 3758 it had been earmarked for possible preservation by a group hoping to save the Clevedon branch. Whatever happened, 3681 was steamed again on the 11th when it towed 3758 to Bristol Bath Road shed for storage. Whilst at Bristol both locomotives received some attention and appeared at a depot open day on Saturday

30th April along with Standard 4MT tank 80043 and 8Fs 48760 and 48706, all withdrawn from Green Park and the latter with its "Great Western Society" headboard back in place for the event. In the event both locomotives were sold for scrap shortly afterwards. On Sunday 31st July, 3758 was recorded at Gloucester's Horton Road shed in immaculate condition on its way to Cashmore's scrapyard. I visited this South Wales scrapyard on a regular basis at the time and on one trip that summer I saw the very clean Pannier again inside a building, I hoped it might still be preserved but sadly both 3681 and 3758 were cut up that August.

Ivatt Tank 41283 was also put back into steam after closure, being steamed during the

In the weeks and months after closure the S&D became an enormous adventure playground. On 16th April 1966 boys play in Sturminster Newton goods yard, evidently still in use by a number of businesses. Tim Chapman.

first week after closure, again on Monday 14th, and finally on Thursday 17th. The steamings were all written up on the shed's roster board, and the locomotive had a chalked message on the fireman's side of the cab - "Keep off – fire lit". 41283 was used to shunt the locomotives prepared for onward movement into position ready for haulage to Bristol and its final act was to position itself ready to be taken away by Hymek D7043 on Friday 18th March. All the other remaining steam locomotives were also towed away on that day, Peak class D15 being used for this working. They were taken to Bristol for storage near the former Barrow Road shed, standing there for over a month before they were dispatched to South Wales scrapyards for cutting up.

Southern Steam

The two Standard Class 4 locomotives taken to Blandford by "Biggin Hill" on the night of 6th March were removed on the 18th March, when 4MT tank 80146 was sent up from Bournemouth to collect them. This movement attracted attention, news of the impending journey had spread and resulted in a number of people turning out to see the locomotives pass. Progress was slow, the convoy stopping at stations where those gathered took photographs and "cabbed" the locomotives. Local Roman Catholic priest and enthusiast Father Pedrick cycled down from his home to Bailey Gate station, where he held a short service on the platform, saying prayers and blessing the two locomotives before they continued their journey. The Broadstone signalman became increasingly concerned at the delay, as driver Johnny Walker eventually took over three hours to cover the 11 mile trip from Blandford. The locomotives were dropped off in the bay plat-

form at Wimborne, subsequently being moved to the Ringwood scrapyard of Thomas Ward.

An amusing story from this period concerns a driver from Bournemouth depot who regularly worked the remaining freight services. Whilst up at Blandford on a freight, he visited a local garage and ordered some spare parts for his car, arranging to collect them on his next working to the Town. However there was only traffic for Wimborne on the appointed day and none for Blandford. On the return journey the train stopped at Broadstone, and after a conversation with the guard and signalman, the locomotive was uncoupled from its wagons and proceeded to Blandford, where the driver collected his spare parts before running the 11 miles back and picking up his train. No doubt the train guard and signalman had enjoyed a cup of tea or two - the S&D's comradeship and independent spirit was still alive and well even at this late stage!

Milk and Ash

With the Southern Region still using steam, various classes of locomotives continued to work up to Blandford on freight services, and a few "specials" until July 1967, when diesels took over. Another significant source of traffic remaining at this time was milk from the dairy at Bailey Gate, which continued until 1968. A late development on the branch that deserves a brief mention was the construction of a discharge siding on the site of Highbridge Works. This was used to deliver Pulverised Fly Ash from Aberthaw power station, needed for construction of the M5 motorway across the

D6551 runs on to the loop which will take it round the six wheeled van, it will then reverse and pick up the milk tanks in the background for onward transit to London. Tim Chapman.

On July 10th 1971 Type 3 diesels 6606 and 6985 draw a train of empty fly ash hoppers away from the unloading point on the M5 construction site at Highbridge. On the left is a siding for crippled wagons and on the right is the BR operations office, placed on the former S&D platform.

Rev. John Sutters, courtesy Phil Sutters.

Somerset Levels. Completed in April 1971, a new junction was laid from the main line and most of what remained of the Works and station was demolished. Trains were double headed by English Electric Type 3 diesels hauling modern hopper wagons and ran until completion of the contract in August 1971. Milk trains continued to run to Bason Bridge throughout all of this, eventually finishing in October when the M5 works finally cut the link.

The Jet Age

An interesting development took place in the spring of 1968, when Bristol Siddeley engineers took over the Down tunnel at Winsor Hill in order to test an Olympus jet engine to destruction. The tests were required following an Olympus engine failure on a Vulcan jet where a turbine wheel had broken out of the engine with catastrophic results. The location was deemed a safe place to carry out these tests, so after permission had been granted from British Rail and the locals, a test rig was built fifty feet in from the mouth of the tunnel. This was a complex business, involving contractors, electricians, testers and instrument fitters, and the installation of scaffolding, high speed cameras and extensive sandbagging. Four tests were undertaken between July and November 1969. In each case the engines were tested to destruction by cutting off the oil supply to the lubrication systems. From the results of these test runs, engineers were able to modify the design of the Olympus jet engine.

Writing some years later, Mike Lethbridge, the development test engineer in charge of proceedings recalled that after the initial test run the inside of the tunnel was "nice and dry". On a visit to check noise levels at surrounding properties, a farmer's wife said she had run into her kitchen to see why her

An Olympus jet engine mounted in Winsor Hill tunnel, four engines were tested to destruction on the site from 1968 to 1969.

washing machine had started on its own, only to realise that it was the whine from the engine in the tunnel. After the tests the tunnel was sealed and a notice was later put up saying "Do Not Enter – Contaminated Oil". The tunnel remained sealed until 2008, when the doors were taken away and people were once more able explore the interior.

Further Reading

A detailed account of the decline of remaining freight services over the S&D and the story of the many demolition trains required to dismantle the line is complex and beyond the scope of this book. If any reader wishes to know more then I recommend Tim Deacon's excellent "The Somerset & Dorset, Aftermath of the Beeching Axe" (Oxford Publishing Company) which records this aspect of the S&D in great detail. "The Last Years of the Somerset & Dorset" (Ian Allan) by Colin Maggs is another excellent source of both information and pictures covering the last years and beyond.

Chapter Six

POSTSCRIPT AND PRESERVATION

WRITING FIFTY YEARS after the event, people still debate the closure of the S&D and the way in which it was handled. It quite possibly had to go, given the climate at the time and the awkward way it sat in the railway landscape, but if it had been intelligently rationalised and had managed to survive, then parts at least would by now be busy passenger operations.

Whilst this will no doubt remain an interesting subject for discussion, the years following closure did see a number of restoration schemes being put forward. As in its earlier history, human frailty, personalities and politics all played their part, and in truth there has been little progress in this direction. And yet at the same time the S&D remains a hugely popular subject amongst enthusiasts, even to many who weren't born until after it had closed.

There have been successes, most notably the preservation of two of the line's famous 7F freight locomotives and more recently a well established preservation scheme on the line at Midsomer Norton. Devonshire and Combe Down tunnels were reopened in 2013 for public use as a walking and cycle route and there are a number of smaller schemes under way along the route, so I hope we may yet see further progress.

Of course the best way to ensure this is to get involved in one of the schemes and actively work for the line's preservation. As mentioned earlier I have long supported the Swanage Railway, which in under thirty years has achieved an amazing renaissance from a bare trackbed to a fully functioning steam railway, with firm plans in place for re-connection to the National Network.

I hope you have enjoyed this book and my efforts to bring back to life the last weeks and days of this most famous of West Country railways. If I have missed anything or you have any additional information then I will be very pleased to hear from you via my publisher.

On Sunday 5th March 2006 Preserved 7F 53809 is on display at Green Park station to commemorate forty years since the closure of the S&D.

Steam returned to the S&D in 2005 when Jinty
47496 visited the developing preservation scheme
at Midsomer Norton, seen here in steam at the
down platform.

TAILPIECE

In the weeks leading up to the closure we paid more regular visits to the line at weekends including taking the train from Bath Green Park to Wellow. On the penultimate Saturday morning, along with my father and sisters, we visited Midford Signal Box and were invited inside by the signalman. You couldn't fail to feel at home with all the shining brass, coloured levers and paraphernalia. I was invited to choose a tablet holder and to my lasting regret chose a small modern and practically unused leather pouch that fitted the Whittaker apparatus, rather than an antique and oiled leather hoop version.

The final Saturday is etched in my memory and cemented by the photographs my father took that weekend; early morning at Combe Down Tunnel and Tucking Mill, the GWS Special at Midford Goods, the spectacle of the two Bulleid Pacifics crossing Midford Viaduct and the last service train on which a friend was travelling.

The picture shows Caroline, John and Janette in Midford signal box on the morning of the 27th February, John is holding the tablet holder that he has just been given.

John Froud

I was a sixteen year old apprentice engineer whose weekends were full of chasing the ever declining steam action around the country. Along with my friends and our cameras, we tore across the Mendip Hills on that Saturday in March, the last day of service over the S&D route.

I had been an enthusiast for as long as I could remember and now with twenty or more cars tearing along in a frantic convoy, the mood was electric. Ahead was the unmistakable 1950s Midnight Blue Mk VI Bentley of Ivo Peters, the famous railway photographer who we all admired.

After a long and hectic day we stood in awe to see the very last service train at Templecombe, the locomotive adorned with a wreath. The "last post" played as we pulled out for Bath that night, making the hairs on the backs of our necks stand up. We all felt we were witnessing the end of an era for steam and the end of our boyhoods.

Michael J. Chapman